B*itten by Sp*ain

Deborah Fletcher

NativeSpain.™com

First Published in 2008 as *Spiders & Wine* by Trafford Publishing

This edition published in Great Britain 2009 by NativeSpain.com

© Copyright Deborah Fletcher

Cover illustration by Debbie Jenkins

Typeset in Book Antiqua

For John, without whom nothing like this would ever happen, and for Ben and Rach, for all their support now and in the future...

Praise For This Book

With a great deal of humour, Debs describes life in a remote valley, while she and her husband are renovating a shed into a liveable house with all the modern commodities necessary for us Northern Europeans. All the while their Spanish neighbours are watching, shaking their heads.

Wild life, in the form of spiders, wild boars and scorpions; pets - whether dogs, cats or cockatoos; neighbourly courtesies, being over-the-fence exchange of produce or at special occasions, are all things anybody who has settled among the Spanish in a rural environment can relate to. Debs describes it with a wonderful sense of humour – aiming both at our peculiar set ways as well as our hosts'.

It is easy reading, full of humour and love for the Spanish way of life. I enjoyed reading it because it is the first book I have come across that I can relate to after 12 years of sharing my life with the Murcians.

Read it – it is a true description of rural Murcian life from an expat's point of view!

Biggy Marshall, Murcia

A book I read avidly, having started greedily after shelving the current. Hard to put down as it's like being there! It's a well written book full of interest and humour.

Paul Spooner

I could have read this book in one go but I savoured it over two sessions. It was brilliant. Wish it was longer! Look forward to the next one.

Shari Ferari

Your book arrived, and I dived straight into it and forgot to make the old man any dinner . It's a really good read, and it's just as if I was listening to you on the phone - you write so descriptively and confidently that the pages just fly by! I have pretty much decided that there are far too many spiders and nowhere near enough wine for my liking, and that you have achieved what most women would have nightmares about!

Susan Beck

Both Sonia and I so very much enjoyed reading Deb's book, Spiders and Wine. Neither of us could put the book down. It was so entertaining with many laughs and quite a number of things we so easily identify with.

Jim and Sonia Bishop

Foreword

This book covers many of the humorous aspects of living temporarily in a static caravan in the Murcian campo whilst trying to create (illegally, as it turned out) a home from an old casita! It describes many of the Spanish habits and foibles, the surroundings, the climate, and all the wildlife with which Deborah herself co-exists, including her ever increasing zoo of parrots, dogs and cats.

This book is an interesting, funny and realistic story of a British couple and their move to the north-west area of Murcia, the trials and tribulations, good happenings and the kindness of neighbours, along with the inherent difficulties and the anticipated joys of moving to sunny, complicated, sometimes frustrating but always fascinating Spain.

Anyone interested in Spain, moving to Spain or who has actually moved here will enjoy this well written and absorbing account, which grew out of Deborah sending emails to friends and family detailing her daily happenings and all the ordinary and not so ordinary things which make up the life of this ex-pat couple.

Anyone who enjoys a good read particularly about the love affair the British have with Spain (albeit sometimes a love-hate relationship) will enjoy this book!

Clare Smith , The Reporter

Contents

Introduction

We decided to make the move to sell up in the UK and buy in Spain earlier than originally intended after we were rudely awoken by the smack-around-the-head recognition of our own mortality following the loss of a few friends to sudden and unstoppable illness; also, on my part, because the business I had run for some ten years was sucking the very life out of me.

John, however, loved (still loves) his job as a firefighter and trauma technician with Greater Manchester fire brigade, and opted to remain employed by them. This had four obvious benefits. First, he would continue to earn a better wage than we could hope to achieve in Spain, even after costs. Second, he could maintain his fire brigade pension scheme and retire at around fifty-two (okay, still some eighteen years hence at that time but a whole lot earlier than most people nonetheless). Third, it took the pressure off him learning to speak Spanish – he is not, by his own admission, any sort of linguist and it was his biggest fear throughout all the preliminary discussions. Fourth, we would be apart for almost half of the time, which never seems a bad idea in any relationship, if you ask me.

So we bought in Spain at the end of 2003. The first place we bought (and this was entirely John's fault) was a very nice villa with pool and jacuzzi in a small but developing village called Sucina some fifteen kilometres inland from the Mar Menor coast.

I was more unhappy there than I can begin to tell you.

I had always said that I wanted a finca inland, to grow my own produce, to keep chickens, and to afford sufficient room to house my passion (my pets).

"No," said John, "I don't want you stuck out in the campo on your own when I, your knight gallant, am not there to defend you." (Oh, someone get me a bucket, please).

However, nagging will out – and about two years later, we bought a large piece of land, more than seven acres in area, with a small ruined casita on it and a huge old barn. The land is steeply terraced, with the remains of an almond plantation still staggering along its various levels, which extend from the barn at the very top and descend down the south-facing side of a valley to the river Mula that marks our lower boundary.

It is a breath-takingly beautiful area, and needs a scary amount of work to make anything of it.

And I lived in a static caravan while the casita was being turned into a house sympathetic to the other rural constructions around and about.

Alone when John is working, (well, apart from two dogs, a cat and six parrots, plus no end of spiders), and far from old friends and family, with no neighbours to speak of, I began to send out weekly e-mails as a sort of hybrid diary–newsletter …

Darkness

At around midnight, here in the small and flimsy tin can that I laughingly call home, I found myself staring into the eye of the most spectacular electric storm.

In the amphitheatre of the valley, with its tiered seating rising steeply from the river, I was perched up on the rim with the gods. Right under my nose, Thunder and Lightning were playing out a great domestic battle with such intense passion that it seemed as if they were about to destroy each other as I bore witness.

Each searing stab of painful white light sizzling through the torrential rain was met simultaneously by a furious and ear-rending explosion of utter fury. The main characters were supported superbly by the special effects crew, with the ground quaking and rumbling ominously below me and with backing vocals provided by the insane howling of the wild winds. It was a truly inspired and Oscar-worthy all-round performance.

Each crash sounded like a new and bigger piece of scenery had shaken loose and earthed itself on my roof. The caravan was rocking in the gale, with the outrigger chains (with which John, thankfully blessed with foresight, had secured it to the ground) creaking and groaning alarmingly. Without these, I feel sure that the raging elements would have flipped the whole thing over like a pancake and sent us tumbling down the terraces and into the river below.

The dogs were in the caravan with me. Jade, our German shepherd, wetting herself with bravery, was trying to sit on my lap and bury her head in my armpit, as she tends to do when assaulted by any loud noise. Qivi, our husky, slept on in total oblivion, with such complete disregard for the furious forces outside that he was snoring loudly in counterpoint to the thunder. Smokie, the diminutive cat that owns us, had at the onset of the storm disappeared rapidly into the long barn, which she regards as her safe haven, and stayed there – probably tucked up under a tarpaulin covering an armchair. It was raining so hard that I couldn't even consider checking on the poor parrots, locked away in the middle barn and with the din on its tin roof probably scaring them all even more witless than was already the case.

Then with a grand flourish, a triumphant climactic lightning strike knocked out my electricity.

It is pretty hard to imagine the darkness that envelops all things here in our valley in the campo when the very few artificial lights dotted around are extinguished. With no light pollution from civilisation, and not even a glimmer of moonlight through the clouds, I was rendered utterly sightless.

So I tentatively fumbled my way around the caravan, searching for the couple of night lights I remembered having put somewhere handy just in case. I managed to send just one plastic tumbler flying with a carelessly-placed hand, and I trod on Qivi's tail and then fell over him as he reared up, but I did find the candles. I huddled round these feeble sources of light for an hour or so, much too cowardly to attempt the fifty-metre walk to the main fuse box at the other end of the barns. I regularly get zapped by cars, cats and iron gates – I didn't fancy my chances in any stray lingering lightning, what with the ground sodden below me and raindrops like water bombs falling steadily. And I was thinking, "please, please, please, pretty please with a cherry on top let it just be the trip-switch", not some serious full-system burn-out. I've already had one mad dash to pick up an emergency electricista from town for what turned out to be a false alarm (the main wire into the fuse box had come adrift, having not been fixed properly by the first electricista) – not my fault but it didn't make me very popular at the time, nonetheless.

Fortunately, the little oven in the caravan is gas-fired, so I was able to fortify myself with coffee and Ponche Caballero until I was totally convinced that Thunder and Lightning had finally decided to kiss and make up, and I felt it safe enough to charge through the deluge of rain to discover that it was indeed merely the circuit-breaker.

My flock and I heaved a collective sigh of relief, as we settled down to doze for what remained of the night, soothed by the now soft and steady rainfall in the period of calm following the storm.

Neighbours & Eggs

We met our neighbours recently. They are only part-time neighbours in that they live elsewhere in what I imagine to be great comfort and civilized surroundings during the week, and then arrive en masse for the weekend to slum it and to play at being country folk.

Last Sunday the head of the household, a large and menacing-looking chap, bellowed something fiercely through the fence to John in a manner that brought to mind an enraged bull. John, in his habitual fashion, looked pathetic and panicky, and desperately tried to attract my attention, but I was hiding in the barn struck with sudden deafness, determined that he should at least make an initial effort to manage alone.

Anyway, after much gesticulation our neighbour managed to communicate his wish to John that we should go around to share a cafelico with him and his family so that we could get to know each other. So off we trotted obediently to make the acquaintance of the noisome and ferocious Pedro and his pleasant and friendly wife Loli, plus the rather droll Pedro Junior (even bigger than Papa) and sweet and sunny little Luisa, all keen to make welcome these new and strange alien beings that had landed in their midst and had decided (insanely) to make the campo their home.

First we were shown around their very pleasant country retreat. An ongoing barn conversion, being carried out tastefully little by little each weekend, it boasts three rooms – a lounge, a large kitchen and a bathroom – together with a big open space destined to become two bedrooms. With white-washed walls and natural stone floors, it has a pleasant and airy feel to it, and has been cleverly furnished in a complementary rustic style with old wooden furniture and home-grown rugs.

The high timber mantel shelf above the wood-burner in the lounge, along with the ornate plate-rail running around the walls at head level, and the large knarled dresser, and in fact every other available perch, is filled with lovingly-restored items of antiquity. It is their passion to hunt down and return to splendour all manner of old and interesting oddities, Loli told us proudly, as she waved in rapid succession under our noses a brass miner's lamp, a beautiful and intricate fan-shaped fire guard, and an inlaid mahogany ashes casket.

We obviously made all the right noises of appreciation, because we were taken warmly to their bosoms as Pedro declared repeatedly the importance of good neighbourliness, friendship, much shared wine and mutual assistance. All fine and splendid, I think – we would very much appreciate good neighbours and do try our utmost to reciprocate, we are very friendly little bodies and we're always ready to share a glass or two of vino tinto. I may however be a little less sure of the last item on the list – Mutual Street so often turns out to have been made one-way by the town planners. But we'll see.

Loli had already started to prepare coffee, and its freshly-brewing aroma suffused the air while Pedro ushered us into the back yard and garden to look at all the beautifully-manicured fruit trees, so very much at odds with our own, and to meet his handful of chickens. I mentioned that I intended to keep chickens too, when the house is finished, which delighted Pedro, who proceeded to rummage around underneath various indignant hens to look for eggs.

He managed to recover just one solitary egg between the six hens, which didn't impress him much at all: however, with good grace, he turned and presented it proudly to John for la cena – his supper.

We then returned to the terrace area, which faces directly towards the east (and, coincidentally, the caravan – we couldn't have sited it any better to give the neighbours full view of our antics even if we tried). We sat enjoying a fresh breeze in the shade below the rough canopy thrown over the wooden framework of the porch on the terrace, and drank hot and strong coffee followed by tumblers of home-produced wine. Deep red and fruity, we were informed that this wine was made entirely without additives, and would therefore never leave behind the unwelcome hangover.

We spent about two hours sipping comfortably, while we were regaled with accounts of the production of great feasts in the huge wood-fired oven just below the terrace, and of scorpions lurking under rocks waiting to find an empty shoe in which to squat, and about the paellas cooked to celebrate the coming of thousands of snails after rainfall, until finally we took our leave, slightly inebriated and feeling warm and loved.

John reached out to shake Pedro's hand … and dropped the egg.

Embarrassing? You have no idea!

Drivers & Drunks

We went out to the local Tuesday street market recently to stock up on the fruit and vegetables that we're not yet at the point of producing ourselves.

I regret the need to confess that we have recently bought the ultimate item of shame for such market visits, in the shape of a dreaded Rolser shopping trolley – Burberry-clad, even. This purchase was made according to the logic that it would prove much easier on the hands than are the tourniquets that masquerade as handles of ever-extending plastic bags full of heavy produce. And anyway, it seems to be the only way to avoid mortal damage at the hands of all the old ladies with their own trolleys – a case of their ankles or ours, really.

In actual fact, it is John that normally drives it – and I do use the term loosely. Personally, I would meekly drag it along behind me, but John charges into the fray pushing it ahead of himself, like some sort of lance-shield combo. He has even suggested, uncharitably, that we mount horizontal blades on the wheels in the Boadicaea style, for extra effect.

And it's tempting…

Anyway, we do seem to get through the gossiping hordes quicker these days, I have to say, which (possibly) partly makes up for the sheer mortification of actually owning such a thing.

So we arrived back at the barn expecting to be greeted by the two hounds of the Baskervilles baying loud and long at the gates in their usual fashion – and found only one. Jade was doing her absolute utmost single-handedly, but Qivi was nowhere to be seen.

Having unlocked the gates, I left John to bring in the car laden with its booty, while I ran ahead to locate the missing hound. No sign in his kennel, nothing by the caravan, not a flicker of life anywhere on our terrace or the one below. Beginning to panic, I ran to yank open the barn door.

He tumbled out noiselessly, slid gracefully down the ramp and landed in a heap at the bottom on his chin, eyes closed, brow furrowed, and utterly unable to move further.

When I called his name, he struggled to open one eye, peered at me sorrowfully, and made a piteous little kitten-like mewing sound as he closed it again.

Stricken, I knelt down by his side in some concern, deeply fearful for this great and proud creature, usually so full of bounce and noise, now looking half-dead. I pulled both eyelids up with my thumbs, but his normally-beautiful steely blue eyes, horribly blood-shot, rolled upwards into his skull.

I stroked his head gently and talked to him in low soothing tones as I dipped my head to lie alongside his mouth, checking for the feel of his breath on my cheek – only to be overwhelmed by a great waft of alcohol.

It transpired, upon further investigation, that in our absence he had rummaged through some of the boxes stored in the barn, including the drinks box, and had found a sealed (and expensive!) gift set of Guylian chocolate liqueur and chocolates.

"Christmas!" he thought, and promptly devoured all of the chocolates. Having thus stimulated his taste buds, he obviously decided that he might as well be hung for a sheep as a lamb, bit off the whole bottom of the (glass!) bottle of liqueur and swallowed the lot.

So I was in fact looking at a dog of the completely hammered variety.

He spent the next twelve hours acting more than a little sorry for himself. His half-lidded eyes were unable to find a focal point other than the end of his own nose, he looked as though his head had been filled with large rocks, and when he walked his gait was that of a dog with twelve knees, articulated in as many different directions.

I encouraged him to drink copious amounts of water, although he was sick almost every time, but I thought that at least it was best to get it out of his system and to attempt to rehydrate him at the same time.

It took him two days to recover fully, such was his hangover. He was incredibly lucky to survive the affair, on a whole raft of counts.

Needless to say, they are now banned from the barn, despite the weather.

Morning Glory

I have never in my life seen such rain!

In fact, if I'm totally honest I didn't see most of it, as much of the time the cloud was actually enveloping the caravan like wet cotton wool and I struggled to see much beyond the door. For a week, I resorted to bringing all nine of the animals into the caravan with me so that at least we could all keep warm and dry together. I could of course only get away with this while John was firmly back in the UK for two weeks…

The camino, never in a good state, has turned into a mudslide, and negotiating it by car (which indeed I have not tried for a week, since my last foray for gas and animal food) has sunk to the level of a white-knuckle ride. I slide down the ramp from the uppermost barn terrace towards the camino and the house roof level trying to obey the anti-skid logic and not to apply the brakes but oh-my-god-there's-the-edge and I've almost got my foot through the floor in a Flinstonesque attempt to halt the car. Not to be undertaken by the faint-hearted.

But today at last we have a bright, clear and above all warm day, so let's hope the weather is finally set to improve. I think we've had entirely enough rain to restock the reservoirs by now.

It seemed very strange, but I was awoken this morning by an insistent cuckoo not so very far away from the caravan. Never before having heard this call in Spain, it felt to me, struggling in the twilight of abandoned sleep, for all the world as if I had been carried back to Constable's rural England by the currents of the night.

Of course, we also have the more recognized form of alarm system in the neighbourhood in the shape of Pedro's rooster next door and another across the valley, but they are clearly of the student persuasion and don't shake a vocal chord until about midday.

We also have a pigeon loft on top of the barn. When we first bought the place and investigated its various nooks and crannies, we found an internal chute running down from the superstructure of the pigeon loft into one of the sections of the barn, which we assume had been used for feeding from inside at ground level. Since there were at least half a dozen nesting pairs flitting about in the barn rafters who had decided that they preferred inside to out, we waited until the chicks had fledged and then firmly closed the door. We then shovelled out great heaps of bird poo, which was spread thick like icing on top of years of goat droppings and hay, and sulphur-bombed the whole room to kill off any nasty lurking bugs.

We now use this area as the tool-cum-work shed, but it is not the most pleasant of places to work given that it still reeks of rank goat incontinence.

Anyway, the pigeons, banished to their smaller loft space, were not best pleased. They have recently retaliated by inviting the local Pigeon Clog-Dancing Ensemble to meet and practise on the tin roof of the barn – another delightful early-morning rude awakening. Aaah, country living!

I was informed by our dearest Bullero friend Jose that the 29th of April marks the fiesta of San Marcos here in Bullas. Since John will not be here, Jose insists that I join him at this momentous occasion, along with his family and his right-hand girl from the office, the lovely Nati.

He says that the fiesta will be marked with a big paella and beer to be served at La Rafa centre close by.

Oh, absolutely, I say – to decline would be rude.

Then he tells me that for the parade we must wear costumes of las huertanas, the country women, which look heavy, itchy and uncomfortable, as well as expensive to hire.

Oh. I'm washing my hair all day, I say – to accept would be foolhardy.

However, Nati has whispered in an aside to me that he can go and sing if he thinks we're wearing those horrendous flea-ridden and simply "pasado de moda" things, and that we'll go as we are, thank you so very much.

Hmm… Jose is in fact the local karaoke champion. The jury is therefore still out on that one. I'll let you know.

Almond Trees
& Visiting Boars

We are all feeling very much better here for the dramatic change in weather. And what a change! Yesterday morning I was freezing and had two jumpers on while I cleaned the parrots and gave them their breakfast, and then by the afternoon it was running at 32°C and I was seriously thinking of exposing some horrid white flesh to the clear blue skies. In the event, I merely donned a T-shirt, as I was worried that any overreaction from me might scare the sun away again.

The dogs now have over seven acres of land in which to roam free, but choose instead to spend their entire time right under my feet dropping weapons of toe-stubbing torture in my path for me to throw for them. I habitually lob these offending items down into the thickest undergrowth I can reach so that the dogs fail to find and fetch them. While the dogs try very hard to thwart me, surfacing eventually empty-mouthed but decorated with a sundry assortment of gorse and wild plants much in the style of deep-camouflage military personnel. The accessories for which I then have to brush out constantly, I might add.

The cat, having spent some weeks wallowing in agoraphobia and hiding under the tarpaulin in the long barn, has finally decided that it's actually quite a good place in which to be totally at liberty, and has taken to performing sentry duty up and down the rock wall supporting this top terrace. I haven't yet seen her go further, but I'm keeping an eye out since there are at least half a dozen cats, all bigger and harder than her, that appear to belong to the three properties closest to us and who probably feel they have a prior claim on the land, as it was unoccupied for so long.

John has finally come to the point of full agreement with me with reference to residing in the country. His attitude thus far really has been that of "I'm not entirely sure why we have to do this but if it keeps the old bat happy…"

On Tuesday, however, before we made the run to Alicante in the evening to send him back to the UK and to work (there but for the grace of John go I), he confessed that he was utterly loving it and didn't really want to leave, after having spent the day wandering about the land with his gardening tools (that is, a petrol chainsaw) and pruning the ranks of almond trees.

As well as olive and fig trees, which look after themselves very well without much human intervention, we also have something like a hundred almond trees dotted about all over the various terraces. These have never been irrigated, and have obviously had no attention for some eight years since the death of the previous incumbent.

Almonds need to be harvested – if they are left to rot on the branch then they kill it. So these trees are not by a very long chalk at their best. Having said that, we did some work last year on them and they are yielding a reasonable crop this year. The only problem is that what John has in enthusiasm for pruning he lacks in aesthetic sense, so the trees have finished up looking a bit like a line-up of extras from the Texas Chainsaw Massacre...

Nonetheless, we have high hopes, and we are joining the local Co-operative so that we can sell our almonds – apparently they pay around ninety cents per kilo, and last year we harvested about twenty-five kilos from just three trees.

We are told that we can also take along our olives to a mill in nearby Cehegín in exchange for payment or for oil (or a bit of each) so we'll just have to see what it all amounts to.

When we first bought here, we found, as we were walking along each terrace checking accessibility, the carcass of a wild boar – recently deceased. After it had rotted down, I did keep the jaw bone and teeth for a while until Qivi found them lurking about and decided they were a dog treat, thank you so much.

Obviously, then, this is jabalí country. I'm not at all worried by this as I am given to believe that they are quite timid creatures generally, although I'm told that they can be ferocious if cornered. No cornering intended, trust me.

Now something fairly big has started getting through the eastern perimeter fence, so John is working on making it good on the basis that he'd rather exclude whatever it is than deal with its confrontational issues – an attitude I applaud thoroughly.

"Naaah," says Jose, "Just let it come. We'll build a huge barbecue..."

Incommunicado

Sincere apologies for my greeting of the Sun last week. I was so glad to see it that I threw the doors wide, mixed some sangría, put on the music and was generally profusely welcoming. The Rain, just about to leave, sensed the party atmosphere and decided it would be surly to go too soon, and took its shoes back off and re-joined the dance. The Sun has been skulking in the kitchen ever since. My fault.

Before we actually made the great move, we spoke to various people living out in the campo with regard to telephony (as obviously there is no landline, and little chance of same). No problem, we were told – there is a radio phone system available from a company called Iberbanda, which costs around 40€ per month and provides telephony and broadband internet. Wow! We thought – no loss of communication then, and cheaper than Telefónica (but then, so is gold dust).

So we duly signed up and waited for the engineer to come and fit us out.

I had a call from same engineer, Antonio, within two weeks. "I don't know where you are," he said, a little peevishly. "Please come and get me from town."

I therefore had to make the usual bone-shaking trip twice along the camino to get him here…

He climbed out of his van sucking his bottom lip and shaking his head, just to put us thoroughly at our ease, and squinted morosely up at the hill on the opposite side of the valley, grossly, I must say, exaggerating its height as he did so.

Then he got out his incredibly complicated and sensitive signal-testing equipment – vis-à-vis a step-ladder – which he propped against the barn and ascended to roof level. He then peered myopically into the distance in the opposite direction over the barn roof-top, muttering to himself all the while.

When he descended again, it was to pronounce very firmly that, "no", we couldn't possibly get a signal here.

"How can you tell?" I asked.

"I can't see the mast."

With which, he bundled his stuff into his van with improper haste and disappeared back along the track in a cloud of dust.

So, back to the drawing board, it would seem. We discussed satellite telephony with various technicians, but they were generally of the opinion that it would require a small mortgage to fund and still wasn't especially reliable. Our only available option appeared to be a mobile phone contract, and the new "GPRS/3G" mobile modem.

So that's what we have. It's a horrible plastic little thing, smaller than a mobile phone, that allegedly allows the computer to link to the internet at broadband speed – although that is only if you have 3G cover, which we don't; failing that, it will achieve standard GPRS speed (a.k.a. watching paint dry).

We have very little choice – it's that or nothing.

My problem is that it is a severely lazy little modem – when I boot it up, it will open one eye and peer at the sky. If there are clouds to be seen, it glares at me and says, "You must be kidding," and goes back to sleep, not to be roused again until the next clear blue sky day (which are few and far between, for now).

I must just take a moment to say, though, that despite the trials the weather has so far thrown at us, I really do love it here. Yesterday evening, during a mild sunny spell, I sat for a while outside the caravan at the top of the land, sipping a glass of excellent Bullas wine and reading quietly.

Overhead, large birds of prey were swooping down from the prominent rock on the opposite side of the valley and gliding effortlessly on thermals along the whole length of the cut. Their graceful passage caught my eye, and I watched them for a while, an observer unobserved. Then, glancing down into the valley towards the river and up the other side at the neat terraces of almond trees and the pine forest beyond, all looking lush and green after the rain, I had one of those deep breath moments where you can't quite believe it's all real…

Self-Sufficiency & The Arrival of Marcos

We ate the first pound of fresh, firm and deliciously-sweet strawberries from our own plants for breakfast this morning. Actually, no, I tell a lie – strictly speaking, Cookie ate the first pound… and most of the peas, and the tops off about half the carrots before I got a look-in.

That'll be cockatoo pie and spinach for supper, then.

As a matter of fact, we find that we are going to have to fence off the little garden patch anyway, to deter a marauding puppy…

I did attend the fiesta of San Marcos on Sunday, though not in costume – Nati held out. In the event, I felt hideously conspicuous out of costume amongst all the other participants dressed for the part, but never mind – I'll know for next year.

We joined Jose's "float", which was actually a cart and tractor heavily disguised under all manner of bits of local flora and streamers, sound equipment worthy of a major rock festival, and a ridiculous number of cans of beer. We spent the morning dancing and generally being very silly around the entire town to extremely loud latino music accompanied by the regular explosion of the small mortar bombs that pass as firecrackers here. There was an abundance of freely-available alcohol on every float, liberally exchanged, and plenty of snacks proffered for those of a more carnivorous bent than I. Flags fluttered merrily in the very pleasant breeze and all was exceedingly colourful and festive.

I still have the blisters to prove it. It was great fun – most of the local youth were falling down drunk by midday, with their white huertano costumes heavily splattered in red wine (and not one good detergent commercial in sight...) but it was very warm despite the breeze, and I am unaccustomed to such vigorous morning exercise, so I just drank water.

When we got back to La Rafa centre for the paella, I saw, amongst the heaving masses thronging about between the temporary bars and food stalls, the tall thin figure of our local postmaster wandering about bearing a huge and floppy puppy in his arms, asking all and sundry if they wanted to offer him a home, including me.

I said no...

...so, his name is Marcos, in honour of the Saint on whose day I got him. He's only about six weeks old, and already the size of a small collie. Alfonso our vet says he's a cross-bred Spanish Mastín (i.e. a humungous bugger) but it must be said that he is exceedingly cute at the moment – all big eyes, wispy fur and needle-like teeth. Alfonso himself has a full-grown, pure-bred male, he tells me, that stands at waist height and weighs in at some seventy kilos!

"Don't worry," he says, "Marcos is not pure-bred – he'll probably be smaller than that."

Not if he's crossed with a donkey, he won't.

John, informed of this development when I next picked him up from the airport, said, "Oh, good."

Not.

Amongst a very large number of other things.

We've spent a few days hacking down some of the undergrowth on the top level of the land near the caravan, following dire warnings by Pedro next door of all the poisonous spiders and snakes likely to be lurking therein. He graphically demonstrated by the raising of his forearm with clenched fist atop just how big and thick the snakes can be (but surely not that hairy?)

I'm really not bothered by creepy crawlies, but we felt it would be a neighbourly gesture to show just how seriously we take his abundant advice.

He also warned us about lighting fires to dispose of the waste (although we don't intend to do this anyway – we're going to compost). He said quite firmly that we must watch for the published dates for burning, because if we tried it out of season then "Los guardabosques te comen!" (the forest rangers will eat you).

That's if the spiders and snakes don't get us first.

The Onset of Tractors

Okay, the saga of the phone continued recently when my friend Donna, who lives about two kilometres away on the westward side of the Bullas mound, mentioned in passing that although she wasn't able to have the Iberbanda phone either, they could at least fit her with broadband internet, as it can function with a weaker signal than the phone, apparently.

So in true British style we got back onto Iberbanda and said, "Oi! Why were we not offered this option?"

It therefore transpired that, in the true cyclic nature of all things, I went to meet Antonio (another one), dragged him out here along the ruts and furrows that are our camino, and asked him to test for a signal for internet.

He started immediately into the old head-shaking routine, but I pre-empted him this time by shoving an ice-cold bottle of beer into his hand while John put our ladders up against the barn just to make sure he wouldn't be flitting without fitting.

With orders sotto voce to the dogs to make sure that he kept his feet well off the ground until further notice, we more-or-less herded him to climb up the ladders and onto the roof and then further up to the pigeon loft, which he duly did; this time armed with a proper signal testing box and an aerial, and looking, I have to say, far more promising than the last guy.

There ensued various loud squeaks and grunts and other best undescribed emissions from this box. After listening for some ten minutes in rapt concentration, he finally whistled for our attention and raised both thumbs to us. "Yes," he said, "They can see you very clearly. You could even have a phone!"

Hallelujah! So now I have superquick internet and (all things being equal) a phone on the way.

Now it is a known fact here amongst the folk of the campo that only the truly deranged or the British actually want to live in the campo. All the Spanish have houses elsewhere and just keep a little place out in the wilds for weekends and holidays, for a spot of gardening, ginormous barbecues and serious amounts of family noise. Oh, and a chance to get out the old tractor.

It is hard to negotiate the streets of this town at weekends, thanks to the tractor brigade.

If you think it's annoying sitting in a car waiting for two cars in front of you, parallel-parked in the middle of the road, to finish their discussion through open windows about Magdalena's illegitimate baby, or the antics of the new priest, or the entertaining shapes of Señora Lopez' carrots, then you should try it behind two (or more) tractors, discussing some variation on the theme but belching out clouds of smoke and often towing trailers of sh... (you know what) to boot.

The tractors vary from the brand new gleaming expensive state-of-the-art machines to heaps that give hitherto unknown and shameful meaning to the word "dilapidated", but the men that drive them are all much of a muchness – luxuriant black moustache, cap, beer belly, clothes that look better suited to a scarecrow, fat cigar.

We are aiming to join them soon (although I draw a line at the cigar and would also struggle with the moustache) when we take delivery of our long-awaited machine. More of that later.

I must just say, though, that all this recent unseasonal rain has caused some consternation amongst the tractor brigade, who clearly still feel the need to fire up the old girl and give her a run, but have precious little to do in a downpour. I can always tell a Saturday in the rain here – you can't get within five hundred metres of a bar for the plethora of parked tractors outside.

Or, given that they are Spanish tractors, perhaps they are just getting in the fortifying first whisky of the day?

The house, I am pleased to report, is only a couple of days from completion of the external works, although the huge change in weather from cool and wet to total meltdown has resulted in a simultaneous slowing down of the workforce, so I may be a little optimistic.

However, the next round of battle commences soon as we seek quotes for the work for all the services. Electrical wiring is always an interesting one, because any Spanish electrician will look utterly bemused if you tell him you want at least half a dozen plug sockets per room, extra fuseways for outside lights, electric gates etc., plus, in our case, lights to animal enclosures.

(Why? Animals see in the dark. Yes, but I don't!)

Add to that the need for individual switches and a master for all the persianas and we have much tutting and nodding, indicating an urgent need to speak to the bank manager in order to consider such a bizarre and frankly foreign system.

Then the plumber finds he has to get all the waste in to fit seamlessly with the schematic from the underfloor heating engineers, and "¡Madre mía!" The British are clearly as insane as we have always suspected.

We are continuing to clear bits of land (slowly, with just a hoe and a rotavator) in order to keep Pedro's hungry wildlife at bay, but are in truth dragging our heels because the tractor will make such light work of it. The area surrounding the caravan now looks fairly civilised – the ground is gravelled, and we have a table and chairs out on the edge with a large umbrella overhead. A free-standing double hammock stands in the shade of one of the fig trees, while we have two garden bench seats under another. I have planted Russian vine and various cactuses in a huge stone-walled tub that John has built around the base of the electricity pylon standing at the centre of the terrace edge, to soften its utilitarian aspect.

John has also managed to find time to build a small barbecue near the caravan (of size designed to accommodate chicken drumsticks rather than boar), and so we are now thoroughly enjoying the warm dusky evenings inhaling the mouth-watering aroma of barbecue mixed with the wafting scents of wild herbs and pine, with citronella candles and early stars flickering softly in an otherwise light-free zone, with the sound of the burbling river below providing a soothing backdrop to the industry of the crickets and toads. Accompanied by a glass or two of heady red wine, it really doesn't get much better than that, does it?

27

Murcian Spanish
& Bonfires

If anyone ever describes the campo as peaceful and tranquil, just laugh outright in their face. With the weather suddenly turning ridiculously warm for this time of year, I have needed to open wide as many apertures in this caravan as possible, unless I wanted to discover first-hand how it would feel to be cooked slowly in a tin can. Hence I can say that I've been up close and personal with the campo nightlife, and am therefore fully qualified to state that it is BLOODY NOISY!

Between the croaking of toads, the calling of night birds, the brief squeaks of small animals meeting their demise, and various and sundry other honking, ticking, screeching, gargling and farting noises (actually, that's probably the dogs), it is, in fact, damn near impossible to get any sleep whatsoever.

Talking of leaving the caravan well-ventilated, I confess that for a few nights I actually left the door wide open. And yes, I've had more than enough earache about it, thanks anyway.

My perfectly-sound and logical reasoning for this was two-fold. Firstly, it was pretty airless for about a week and I really did need to cool the place down, and secondly, I have a large and very leaky puppy, whom I don't like to shut out entirely given that he regularly falls down the steps of the caravan and I therefore wouldn't trust him in the pitch black with the terrace edge. He was therefore allowed to sleep inside the caravan but had ready egress in his (many) times of need.

Well, anyway, that's all changed now. Partly because it has cooled down again quite dramatically at night, but mainly because when I woke up on Sunday morning it was to find that he had managed to get into a drawer in the caravan so that when I looked outside it was to be met with the vision of the terrace gaily festooned with the majority of my underwear.

I actually have to use my feeble Spanish rather a lot here. If I want anything at all it's unlikely I can get it without. I have to confess, though, that I am becoming quite fond of the Murcian bone-idle way of giving voice to the Spanish language, where they swallow half a word, never say "s" and substitute "c" for "t" with alarming regularity. Why? 'Cos it means I can be lazy too!

I don't have to worry about the need to be formal or informal when addressing someone new as no-one would ever know if the "s" is not pronounced at the verb ending anyway! It saves many a social faux pas.

And I'm really getting to like one aspect of communication that I came across rarely in the Sucina area but is an integral and essential part of conversation here – the head-shake tut!

As in, "Do you have a loaf of bread (in this bread shop) please?"

"No" (tut).

I used to think the tut translated as "of course not now please get out of my face you horrible British nuisance."

But now I realise that it's actually merely a clarification of and accent upon the word "no".

So I'm enjoying its use myself now. When Francis, our builder, asked me the other day if his recent quote for a paltry forty-five metre section of our camino to be resurfaced was of interest, I could answer firmly, "No" (tut).

Which he would take generally to mean "No", but which I can tell you in fact translates as, "No not on your life it's wildly exorbitant beyond belief and hell will freeze over before you get the job."

A very satisfactory part of speech, the tut.

Things are moving on well. We now have a phone. Okay, so it was a torturous route, but we got there eventually.

The other torturous route (utterly beyond belief, actually) has been the acquisition of the tractor.

You probably wouldn't believe how close I've come to murder on this one. If I see another Farmer's Weekly or Agricultural Gazette or What Tractor? in my life then the reader is likely to end up having to extract it from whatever orifice I can reach first.

Can you begin to imagine what it's like to have your nearest and dearest climb into bed beside you, snuggle up and whisper lovingly into your ear, "Let's talk tractor"?

However, John has survived by the skin of his teeth and the tractor is finally bought; it will arrive here coincidentally just as John starts his long eighteen-day stint. So I don't expect to see much of either of them, in all truth. Though I'm quite sure I'll have things to report...

Pedro next door has been practising what he preaches and has raked most of his pretty wildlife garden into total submission – that is, down to bare earth and rock. The heap of spoil he created was then unceremoniously burnt (it's obviously not forest ranger season, then!) with scant regard for the fact that the wind was blowing in my direction and I got all the smoke. So I had to make a mad dash outside to rescue the parrots, who had previously been enjoying some sunshine and fresh air, and get them back into their barn before suffocation; also to take in my washing, before my clothes and bedding smelt like John's uniform.

Fortunately, much of what grows wild here is of the herb family, so the smoke actually had a very pleasant, if somewhat choking, aroma.

I shall return the compliment when the wind changes direction – I still have that heap of old hay and goat droppings to burn...

Of Toys & Confused Birds

My mum has always maintained that I am the world's biggest sucker for waifs and strays. It's probably the only subject that she and John agree upon – and then only because he has thus far failed to realise that she also includes him in that category.

My current band of waifs and strays have between them caused me some trouble this week – I'll start with John, the biggest of them and the one that generally gives me the most grief.

We went shopping recently to pick up various and sundry items, but top of the list was a large fridge to put in the barn, mainly to house all the cold drinks required when working outside in this heat.

We left looking for a fridge, and came back with…

…a cement mixer.

Now I blame myself for this. I am so very aware that moving here to live in primitive conditions in order to carry out huge amounts of back-breaking work and leaving behind a very civilized and completed villa was not John's idea. I have therefore compensated greatly (okay, some call it unashamed bribery) by allowing him to buy a great number of toys.

He now owns a tractor, a digger, a trailer, link box, posthole borer and cement mixer (all on top of his existing and already extensive collection).

So we have reached the point where I need to say no!

And I had occasion to say no firmly for the first time yesterday when he wanted to buy a petrol chainsaw (he already has one, remember), but this one was mounted on top of an extension pole, to prune the tops of trees. This was never in the budget, and only occurred to him because he saw it, so I said no. You can guess – the bottom lip started to tremble and I had to drag him off to distract him at the diesel engine oil sweeties counter.

I'm just waiting for the full-blown, face-down-on-the-floor temper tantrum.

Watch what a slap he'll get then.

I have hormonal birds. Pickle, my little blue female lovebird, laid six eggs just before we moved here but they were empty. I'm not really surprised – she's set up nest again and spends her entire time crouching down in front of Sweetpea, the yellow male, in a classic come-and-get-me pose, while he is far more interested in preening himself, and regurgitating for and mounting his yellow air-flow golf ball.

In the meantime, Lucas, the green orange-winged Amazon (who is, incidentally, some six times the size of a lovebird) has decided that he's irrevocably in love with Sweetpea (who is male!) and spends his entire time squatting on top of the lovebirds' cage looking longingly at him and getting his feet bitten by Pickle for his trouble.

Being only partially flighted, generally all the parrots are, when in the barn, out of their cages, apart from the lovebirds who are fully-flighted. On Friday I was doing a full cage strip-down and disinfect so I had the barn door shut and they were all loose. The lovebirds enjoy flying about in the rafters and playing hide-and-seek – it gives them a chance to stretch their wings and have fun by dropping well-aimed little packets of poo-bombs on the bigger birds; and they always volunteer to go back into their cage when tired.

So I'm messing about in Cookie's cage, talking to Cookie who is sitting on top and trying to preen my hair, when Sweetpea flies down from the rafters and lands on my head. Lucas, seeing the object of his desire heading my way, and beside himself with jealousy, launches himself from the top of his cage in Sweetpea's direction (top of my head, remember), misses and lands on Cookie's back. Cookie (male) almost lays an egg, Lucas panics and slides off, clutching three large white tail feathers from Cookie, who screeches at the indignity. Jack, the African Grey, blows up like a puffer fish to become eight inches tall and six inches wide, and concurrently lets out an almighty shriek of sympathy mixed with glee. This spooks Sweetpea, who flies down to sit on my hand, closely followed by an incandescent Lucas, who bites a chunk out of my arm on the way past and craps on my trousers!

They stayed in their cages for the rest of the day, while I sulked with the lot of them.

Marcos has doubled in size in the three weeks that he has been here with us, a fact that I am hoping John isn't really noticing much whilst playing with all his toys.

He is needing some firm handling. His mouth is packed full of needles, which he uses constantly to further his growing expertise in ankle acupuncture – walking around outside here must be very much on a par with wading through piranha-infested waters.

He hasn't yet managed to grasp the finer points of nogeroffyoulittlebugger (clearly male, then).

He's already pushing his luck mightily with Qivi, who is not best pleased anyway about being supplanted as new dog on the block quite so soon. The husky is not tolerating the discovery of a little head in his mouth whilst eating, as Marcos does his utmost to snaffle his food from under his very nose. We've had some pretty serious "I'm big and ferocious and could kill you with one snap" growls from Qivi. But Marcos is very feisty and just growls back, only an octave higher. Methinks he is playing with dynamite, and can only hope he's a quick learner.

We have a degree of role reversal in this household, in that John is the one to screech for help when there is a spider/snake/frog etc. lurking somewhere in the house, while I'm the one to trot off to get the requisite equipment for its humane removal.

But even I did a double-take earlier this week when I reached for the cruet from its place alongside the boiler, only to find an enormous spider wrapped around the salt grinder. I kid you not when I say it must have had a span of about three inches, and it was suspiciously stripey-looking, with legs like pipe cleaners. This was only mitigated by the funniest-looking little white triangular eyes that bobbed up and down in unison as if on springs.

Well, anyway, I startled it as much as it startled me, and it fell off the salt pot and into a conveniently-situated empty bowl below, so I was able to grab it quickly and make haste with it outside to drop it over the edge of the terrace.

"You put it where?" quaked John.

"Well, where did you want me to put it?"

"Barcelona," he replied.

Monstrous Puppies, Hungry Spiders & Brats

The vegetable patch has been flattened.

Marcos, who is, I suspect, half mastín, half yeti, half sabre-toothed tiger and half elephant (and yes, thanks, my maths is fine but this is Marcos I'm talking about) is now sufficiently large to get over the two-foot wire netting with which we surrounded the patch, bending it beyond recognition in the process.

Four-foot wire it is, then – possibly electrified.

And I have, as predicted by our omniscient neighbour, been eaten.

About six days ago I went to bed with a very sore and tense patch on my left calf, which, upon examination, showed a violent "triple response" (red centre, white middle ring, bright red outer ring) of diameter some two inches. The next day, the centre had blistered and was sticky. Now, the centre resembles a large cigar burn and there is still a very hard red ring around it. And it hurts. A lot.

I have been electronically nagged to death by Ben, my son, to seek medical advice on this. Now I probably see a doctor once every third blue moon – waiting rooms are my idea of living hell, since I have the patience of a mayfly when it comes to sitting still. So I decided as a first step to go instead to the local farmacia to see if I could resolve this simply.

The pharmacist nodded his sage old silver-bewhiskered head, and tapped his teeth with his pen.

"Es," he pronounced, "Probablemente una picadura de una araña venenosa" (the bite of a poisonous spider).

Sharp intake of breath between the lips from the various and compulsory black widows (señoras, not arañas) in the shop at the time, and a jostling to peer at my bubonic blister, followed by much nodding of the head and high-volume interchange of the "I've-had-one-of-those-but-mine-was-much-worse-than-that" variety.

Apparently the culprit is likely to be a jumping spider or a wolf spider. Possibly even a tarantula, although I am assured that I would in all likelihood have felt the bite of a tarantula at the time, given their size (and presumably the size of their teeth!). Not a black widow (araña, not señora), as it is probable that I would have been carted in on a stretcher in that case.

Anyway, the pharmacist gave me antibiotic cream to administer thrice daily for ten days, with a warning that I was to see a doctor immediately if my leg dropped off, or something like that.

Ben reckons I should invest in a pair of long wellies. I was thinking more along the lines of a visit to Lorca castle to see if they have any second-hand suits of armour. No, on second thoughts just think what could be lurking in one of those...

My dear caring husband has taken to calling me spiderwoman and keeps asking me to run up to the roof of the barn to check the aerial. If he persists, I'll have to bite him...

I must confess in all honesty to looking a little battle-worn. Between the various bloodied scratches from the puppy, parrots' claws, Lucas' beak, thistles, and falls (loose scree is a bugger to walk on), and blisters from spiders and from shoes (I have the most pathetically soft feet in the known universe), added to bruises, which flourish on me at a touch, I could easily get John arrested for battery, should the need ever arise.

When I reported the acquisition of Marcos, my lovely sister Sue in France e-mailed to tell me that I was as mad as an old sheep, and didn't I realise that la gente de Bullas would think that the soft-touch Inglesa at the end of the camino will take on anything? She fully expected me to awake the following morning to the sight of a three-legged goat and a one-eyed donkey tied to my gates.

The reality is, in fact, far worse. No poor disabled animals, which I would gladly take in – no, instead I have a pack of Spanish críos, made up of an ever-changing assortment of my neighbours' offspring and their friends, standing at my gates every weekend and yelling, "DÉBorah! Queremos hablar con COOOOOOOKIE!"

I think even Cookie cringes now.

So they come in and pick their way through a rolling bundle of excited dogs, whom they ignore totally, and make a beeline for the middle barn where they can terrorise the parrots for an hour or so. The three ringleaders are Luisa, Loli's daughter, who is a really pleasant, slightly plump ten year-old who genuinely loves the animals and is going to grow up to be a wonderful and dependable mama. Her cousin Monica, the same sort of age, is one of those dark-eyed sultry young Spanish girls who couldn't give a flying fig for the animals but spends her time here throwing smouldering looks at John; you just know she's going to be massive trouble as a teenager. Then there's Pepe, a cheeky-looking and self-confident little eight year-old boy, who will take on the whole world and suffers perpetually from verbal diarrhoea. All closely followed by their various amigos.

They all say that they want to hold Cookie, but are in reality too scared to do so, so we have a ritual performance in which they proffer a shaking arm just far enough away for Cookie to crane across the gap ready to step up, but not quite reach, all the time trying to copy him in saying "Hello!" but sounding more like Borat.

This continues until Cookie gets fed up with waiting for the arm to come close enough and so throws himself bodily at them, amidst shrieks of consternation and the rapid handing round of the poor bird as though he was an explosive pass-the-parcel. The process is repeated a number of times until I take pity on Cookie and remove him "to sleep now".

This whole scenario occurs at least five times each weekend.

We are planning on wrought-iron electric gates on the slope at the entrance to the barn terrace – I'm currently looking at an amended design with sub-machine gun turrets incorporated.

Any suggestions for antidotes for spider bites and/or children would be most welcome.

The Doctor &
Queue-Jumping

So it would seem that I now have an active crèche running here. Firstly I am inundated at the weekend with the usual selection of kids that accumulate in the three adjacent properties, and then I look across the terraces to find John and Pedro playing together with the dis-tractor. An interesting sight – John speaks barely a word of Spanish and Pedro is equally well-endowed where the English language is concerned.

Nonetheless, in the time-honoured fashion of children thrown together with a common cause, they were managing very well – and it is gratifying, it must be said, to see them sharing toys so nicely.

This morning I was obliged to take my leg to see a doctor, since it is refusing to heal. It hasn't deteriorated, but still it looks less like I have the puncture wounds inflicted by a creature several hundred times smaller than me but more as if I've had a close encounter of the Jaws kind.

I therefore bit the bullet and took a trip to the "Urgencias" section of our local clinic.

This is a huge clinic – there are twenty-odd consulting rooms surrounding a large waiting area racked out with chairs in the manner of an airport, and, just like an airport, the atmosphere is noisy and anticipatory.

I have been assigned (but never yet met) a Doctor who lurks behind door number two. So I dutifully sat behind the handful of patients already waiting to see him, and waited.

And waited...

And waited...

After about half an hour of absolute streams of no traffic whatsoever through his door, he emerged and announced that he was leaving (for lunch? for good? his wife? the country?), and that we were all to go back to the desk to be redistributed amongst other doctors.

This does not inspire in me the confidence I need to share the intimacies of my leg with this man.

Fortunately, I had been talking to a Spanish friend Anna who was waiting to collect a prescription; she, indignant on my behalf, pounced on a passing male nurse and demanded that he attend to me, which he did, rapidly and efficiently.

As always, it's not what you know, it's whom you know!

I am now on a course of oral antibiotics to combat the infection. I also have to return daily for the nurse to change the dressing and apply this paste, which feels like Nitromors and I am convinced is merely there to burn its way through my leg to save them the trouble of amputation.

Talking of waiting, I'd just like to mention the Spanish practice, alive and well here in Bullas, of queue-jumping by frail little old ladies with short-distance sprint records and six elbows apiece, fashioned of wrought iron.

I have waited patiently in line any number of times now for my turn to see the shop assistant/bank teller/ayuntamiento receptionist etc., only to reach the front of the line and have some four-foot tall blur move past and in front of me to grab my spot. I have thus far reacted to this sort of behaviour in a typically British fashion; I merely mutter under my breath and attempt a withering stare, to both of which they are utterly impervious. This has been winding me up as time passes, until I finally decided recently, after a spot of blatant queue-jumping in the local supermarket, that it would be worth taking a stand.

So when a little old lady shoved in front of me a whole four places, leaving me at the back of a queue six people long at the solitary open till, I stated, quite firmly, "Estoy la última."

She glared at me. I repeated myself, and the person in front of me shrank a little. The offender shook her head at me and pointed triumphantly at the hitherto unnoticed full basket of groceries on the floor at her feet – this apparently had been guarding her place jealously while she blithely continued shopping with another overflowing basket of groceries on her arm.

I ground my teeth, but did not feel capable of a long argument in Spanish about the morals of this method of shopping, so I resorted to the flamboyant Spanish open-hand flick accompanied by a disgusted, "Pah!"

She maintained her place, finally paid and left with a small over-the-shoulder smirk, while I was sending up prayers to the god of retribution that the handles of all her shopping bags would break simultaneously on her way out.

Family, Rubbish &
The Uninvited Melon

Well, I'm still sane (I think – and feedback is neither necessary nor desirable) after the trials and tribulations of sharing my caravan with three others for the best part of a week. A process something akin to a chess game in which every move has to be carefully considered in order to preserve all your pieces (limbs, eyes, marbles, your choice).

Ben and Rachel, his beautiful and patient partner, have been exemplary guests. In fact Ben has been driving the dis-tractor about and helping to build walls, while poor Rach was up to her armpits in vegetable preparation for much of the time. Nonetheless, four grown people sharing one tiny shower cubicle and loo, whose door when open crashes into said guests' bedroom door as well as into anyone stood at the kitchen sink, has all the trappings of a poor farce. We did consider trying to measure the available space by swinging the cat, but, wise creature that she is, she made herself scarce – mainly because she does normally like to stretch out to occupy the majority of the lounge area seating, and was immensely put out to find that it was extraordinarily full of bums for a while (and yes, I choose my words advisedly).

It was only for six days.

Unlike the fabulously long time John has been here.

Eighteen solid days of togetherness with my loved one has become an endurance test, I confess, mainly because of the sleeping arrangements (that is, he sleeps and I can't). Previously, upon coming to Spain, we chose to buy two single beds for ourselves, the reasons being two-fold: firstly, I dislike being hot and sticky at night, so personal space in this warm climate seemed like a good idea; secondly, John is only here for about half the time, so I could wash my single bed-linen twice as often as his.

This did actually work quite well, although clearly it's less friendly than a double bed. We had already decided that when the house is finished here we will opt for a super king-size instead.

In the meantime, however, the caravan contains only a very mean double bed.

And John sleeps like an epileptic giraffe.

So I have been awoken countless times these past few weeks with an elbow in the face, or a leaden knee suddenly flung on top of my stomach, or squashed into a triangle of space the size of a generous napkin (folded) as he subconsciously decides that he's too tall to sleep in the bed lengthways and needs therefore to sleep diagonally across it.

Now obviously sleep deprivation can cause one to say bluntly some of the things that one would normally handle more tactfully, so this morning I was compelled to say, and I paraphrase heavily here, that I rather liked the old sleeping arrangements and that single beds might not be such a bad idea again.

"How old are we?" was John's rejoinder, "You'll be wanting separate rooms next."

Not at all. Separate countries sound far better.

I am having a recurring specific memory problem. Obviously here in el campo we have eschewed many of the trappings of civilisation, like mains drainage, a postal service and rubbish collection.

The former poses no problem – we have been obliged to buy a sophisticated domestic residual water treatment plant, or depuradora, as we are not able to have a standard "fossa septica" as we are so close to the river. John and Ben have been building a bund to contain this, by following the line of the existing top terrace that previously petered out half-way across. I was very specific about the aesthetics of this wall, in that I wanted it to weave about like the existing terrace wall – under no circumstances was it to be straight.

They have achieved this perfectly, and I was highly delighted with the outcome – until we had a barbecue yesterday for our neighbours and were asked independently by three sets of people whether they had been hitting the wine heavily whilst building. Hey ho – how frustrating it is to be so artistically misunderstood!

The second item is also easily dealt with – we have a rented apartado de correos in the post office, which I just have to remember to visit occasionally (generally when the very merry widow, a.k.a. my mother, reminds me by asking if I've yet received a postcard from some far-flung corner of the world).

The hitch there is that I can't just slip in, unlock the box, remove any bills and bank statements, and then leave –

the postmaster, remember, was the kind bloke that palmed off Marcos the bull mammoth onto me. He constantly wants to engage me in conversation regarding how big the cachorro precioso is now, and repeatedly asks me to take Marcos in with me to visit him (probably so he can gloat, and then give thanks at Mass for such stupid and gullible people as the British).

No, my real problem lies with the last item – rubbish. Our nearest rubbish collection point is at the very least a kilometre away, and we do seem, with three dogs, a cat and six parrots, to produce a lot of rubbish. I therefore need to drive my rubbish to the bins.

Now, as you know, I go out in my car along the dreaded camino only when strictly necessary (I'm sure my teeth are loosening!) and so I try hard to be efficient and carry out as many chores as possible in one hit. So I'll put three huge bin bags, bursting at the seams, in the back of the car, along with a box of glass bottles for recycling (you know, asparagus jars, mayonnaise jars, balsamic vinegar bottles etc...), and I'll drive into town to the medical centre, bank, post office, supermarket and so on, and then I'll drive home again.

With the rubbish still in the car. Every single bloody time.

It must be a mental blind spot, but I just can't seem to get it right.

Only John was not amused upon opening the car this morning to find it full of fruit flies, so I'm going to have to seek some counselling on this one.

The leg is still milking it for all it's worth. It now resembles a bullet hole, and looks set to eke it out as long as possible and then leave a hideous scar. I'm still having to go to the local centro de salud for a bit of gratuitous torture every other day – scalpel one day, hyrdrofluoric acid the next – but it's stubbornly refusing to heal. I'm not sure what the next stage will be, but it's now getting tedious.

It was only marginally relieved last Tuesday when I rolled up as usual to find that the two female nurses that I've been seeing alternately were both absent and had been replaced by a young male nurse who was a dead ringer for Ben Affleck.

Not bad, not bad – I'm more of a George Clooney type myself, but anything is welcome as a distraction when you're sitting in the waiting room of the Spanish Inquisition. Anyway, this guy insisted, whilst inflicting the usual pain, on chatting to me about music, about David Beckham and about poisonous spiders all at speed in Spanish, despite my mutterings about not speaking Spanish particularly well. Then, as I hobbled out, he threw after me, in perfect English, "Okay, see you!"

Swine. I hope his caduceus withers and dies.

My vegetable patch has taken on a life of its own. It is still yielding plentiful supplies of carrots, lettuce, cabbage, parsley and spring onions that were planted when we first arrived here. I have also more recently planted some cherry tomatoes, full-size tomatoes, courgettes, mint and coriander, all of which are also very healthy and prolific.

But there has suddenly appeared, amongst all of my carefully planned and nurtured greenery, an enormous and rapidly-growing vine-type plant which Pedro assures me is a melon, and which I didn't plant! It's covered in flowers, and looks set to yield a pretty good amount of fruit – but it wasn't there last year, and I certainly haven't been anywhere near it with a melon, or even a picture of a melon, let alone with melon seeds.

I'm wondering if I climb it will I find huge furniture and some golden eggs…?

Deborah Fletcher

Noise & Fruit

Along the valley in an easterly direction towards Mula, there is, just in sight of the caravan on the other side of the river, a large restaurant complex with a salon de celebración called El Castellico, and it is, indeed, like a mini-castle. I am told that the food is excellent but very expensive, and so we haven't actually tried it.

Last weekend they hosted a wedding party of some size – fortunately, I'm relieved to report, not a regular occurrence. We could see in the distance a great many people milling about like ants on the lawns at the front, and could clearly hear the buzz of normal Spanish top-of-the-lungs conversation. When the music started, it could probably be heard in Murcia itself – the peace of the valley was totally shattered. I had mental pictures of all the wildlife crouching in the undergrowth, covering whatever passes as ears with any available appendage, such was the horrific din. It even caused quite some consternation amongst the horses in the stables just across the river.

Then started the fireworks. Mid-afternoon, glaringly-bright sunshine and the Spanish let off fireworks. Such strange behaviour! I'm positive that they are totally disinterested in all the pretty stars, flashes, cascades and colours that we find so attractive. Fireworks are purely and simply regarded by the Spanish as another easy method of big noise production.

Then, to top it all, they indulge in the hideously-annoying custom whereby, upon leaving such a function, they each drive off leaning heavily on the car horn, making the most unbelievable racket.

I am forced to come to the well-observed conclusion that all Spanish are born half-deaf, or at least are quickly made that way by over-exposure to decibels at their mother's knee.

I have found, during the time we have lived in Spain, that it is very difficult to give the Spanish gifts. A very small gesture of sharing or thanks brings back a ten-fold response which leaves you feeling totally outperformed and very unsure of how to respond.

John has already managed to have a few problems with the dis-tractor, the first of which was a spectacular falling-over on a bend. He has subsequently learnt to keep it balanced back-to-front with add-ons, and fortunately he leapt off as it toppled and was unscathed, but at the time it resulted in some diesel entering the pistons and its subsequent inability to start.

Firstly we had to right the thing – just the two of us, nearly a ton of equipment on a hill on a bend– don't even ask how blue the air was, or how near to divorce we were at that moment, but we're very well-versed now in the principle of levers.

We were trying to work out how we could find a tractor mechanic who would actually come out to look at it, since it obviously wasn't going to be possible to move it, when the ever-alert (for which read "terminally nosey") Pedro came to our rescue, having heard the repeated failure of an engine to fire, wandering nonchalantly over to ask if he could help.

He started to fiddle around with the valves without a feeler gauge, sending John into a blind panic with visions of later total wreckage – John was saying, "No, Pedro, no, no, no," at which Pedro merely glared at him over the top of his glasses and gave a prolonged "Siiiiiii, Dhyon" in response.

He then continued blithely to unscrew things here and adjust things there until some twenty minutes later, as John was stood with head in hands and I was trying mentally to calculate the possibility of forking out for another tractor, he turned the starter motor and the engine caught.

He turned aside our effusive thanks with a wave of his hand and wandered back home looking not a little smug.

So naturally, in order to avoid the old one-way Mutual Street syndrome, we tried to show our appreciation by dropping round a small token of our appreciation for his timely intervention. I had the perfect thing – whilst clearing some long grass earlier, we had found an old pistol lurking around, half buried in the mud. It had no guts, but under all the grime it was apparent that it was quite a beautiful piece, with a copper barrel and a wooden handle bearing an intricate inlaid brass plate.

I cleaned it up and oiled the wood, polished the copper and the brass, and presented it to Pedro to add to their already-huge collection of cosas antiguas.

He was, I have to say, delighted – unable to contain his pleasure, he ran round like a sixteen-stone kid pretending to shoot us all. He then fetched a hammer and nail and mounted it proudly above the door.

"Good," we thought, "A successful and well-chosen gift to show our gratitude for his assistance. And we won't feel bad if we need to ask for same again."

The next morning I awoke to find my own bodyweight in fruit – peaches, apricots and nisperos – piled up outside the gate.

"That's to say thanks for the pistol," says Loli.

Bugger – that wasn't the idea at all. Now I feel the need to say thanks for the fruit!

So I manfully struggled in the heat of the caravan to produce some jam, to make good use of fruit we couldn't hope to eat before spoilage. I then dropped round a couple of jars to Loli, with my thanks.

But it wasn't to end there. Yesterday Luisa appeared bearing two huge chocolate marble bizcochos, cooked by Loli in their outside wood-fired oven – the lightest and most delicious cake I have yet tasted in Spain.

Dammit! I guess that next I'll just have to give them the car, or something.

My sister Sue phoned a few days back. We regularly compare notes on the relative ability of Spanish versus French builders to lie through their teeth. She and her husband Chris are renovating a fermette in a little village in the Picardie region of France, while we are of course trying to finish the house here. We both suffer dreadfully from the "I promise that I'll start the work on Monday…" but (aside) "…I didn't say which year, though" syndrome, and it is somehow cathartic to moan about it to each other.

Anyhow, she asked me how the melon plant was faring. I told her that it is growing visibly as I watch it, and is smothered in flowers, both male and female (the female flowers have a very defined globe at the base, about an inch in diameter).

"So you're pollinating them, then?" she asked.

"Huh?"

"Yeah," she said, "Unlike the courgettes that manage very well on their own, with melons you need to pinch off the male flowers, strip back the petals and stuff them into the female flowers."

Oh.

So there's me out in the garden at eleven o'clock at night (under cover of darkness) doing tawdry things to flowers, hoping that she's not just 'aving a larf.

Spanish Builders

I am delighted to say that I am finally able to announce our proud ownership of internal walls in the house. Great cause for celebration – I was beginning to think I was caught in some sort of surreal Groundhog Day timewarp and that it would never really happen.

Fernando, the builder for this particular bit of the project, was being cute – he had a delivery of materials made here on the day that he had originally promised to start, just to lull me into a false sense of well-being, and then didn't show his face on site for a week.

I phoned that following weekend to ask him where he was, and he promised he would start Monday or Tuesday of the next week.

He arrived on the Tuesday and did a whole day's work, just to make me think we were actually next on the list, and then disappeared again for another week.

A further phone call elicited the excuse that he was "in his bed with colic."

Or possibly, for those of us with the developing healthy cynicism engendered by this environment, on one of the other jobs he has running concurrently with ours. Juggling five jobs, spending a day a week on each (just enough to keep it ticking over and prevent the customer from pulling the plug!) seems to be the normal way of fulfilling a contract here.

I must just sidetrack momentarily to qualify the loosely-coined phrase "a whole day's work". This of course means arriving at around nine in the morning after "desayuno" – a coffee and a whisky (optional) on the way in. Then a sacrosanct downing of tools at eleven-ish for a half-hour "almuerzo", or brunch, involving coffee, possibly wine, possibly beer, and tapas – always taken off-site in a local bar with all the other builders working in the vicinity. Back to site for a few hours more until "la comida" beckons at around two in the afternoon, involving a full three-course menú del día blow-out and subsequent digestive break until around five, at which point they can put in a further (sluggish) two hours until quitting for the day at around seven (to go home to "la cena"). This system is irrefutable – I have even found buckets of wet cement with trowels stuck in them lying around abandoned messily while their owners have made off in haste to the bar to fill their two-hourly requirement for ballast. Nothing but nothing stands in the way of these breaks.

Anyway, to resume – I have been delighted this week to see that Fernando's two trabajadores have been slaving away inside the house every day, even if the great man himself has been flitting back and forth like a mother of quintuplets. And as a result, I have internal walls.

Onward into the breech, then. As I have previously mentioned, I am fully aware that getting the walls finished was actually by far and away the easy part – getting quotes for plumbing and electrics is going to be a long, hard, uphill slog.

Spanish tradesmen never want to begin to understand the hare-brained, foreign and, let's face it, nothing short of mental schemes that the weirdo British seem hell-bent on bringing here with them.

Instead, they will state categorically that they have a far superior system to offer (i.e: the same tired old thing they have been fitting since leaving school to follow their particular career path, and, in point of fact, probably the only one they know) and that we would be best advised to discard our silly notions that "may work OK in the UK but are just not feasible here in Spain ... different climate ... better materials ... superior methods of installation ... blah blah blah." Cobblers.

For instance, our chimney design elevation clearly shows a good, chunky, stone-clad chimney – a veritable fat mama of a chimney sat on its ample and comfortable bum.

The builder (Francis, at that point) chose instead to make it a long thin matchstick of a thing that Lowry would probably have been proud to mount on a painting of a factory.

When we asked him to re-do it in the style we had stipulated, he went through the book of excuses regarding its impossibility – weight, stability, functionality, you name it. All obviously total rhubarb since we held out (on his money) until he managed to produce exactly what we wanted, regardless of his multitudinous objections. And do you know what? His wife has confided in me that she likes it very much and intends to work on him to change their own chimney to one just like it. Oh, sweet justice!

Another classic example: we are having solar panels fitted to the roof of the house to supply all our hot water requirements as well as underfloor heating. The system we have chosen is a German one – all the extensive heat calculations have been carried out by our Belgian heating engineers (and I mean qualified heating engineers, not plumbers). The system involves panels that are different from the conventional water-filled tubes in that they are instead filled with antifreeze at -15oC, which basically means that there is pretty much always heat to be drawn from the outside air even if it's snowing (as it does here in Bullas for about a week each year).

Can the Spanish get their ostrich-like heads around this? Can they bananas. If I had a euro for every time a builder has told me that it can't possibly work and that I'll need a boiler as back-up, I'd be as rich as Croesus and could well afford to pay someone else to take all these "cojones" in my stead.

So I am fully expecting a few battles in the next couple of weeks – and, never forget, this will be exacerbated by the fact that I am of course only a mere dim-witted woman with the audacity to think that I can stand up to the macho Spanish builder and tell him how to do his job!

I can't wait.

Okay, I lied.

Organic Gardening & Paternity

Before anything else, I have to say that my sister is a baggage. I received a rather sheepish e-mail from her yesterday admitting that she may have, and I quote, "misled (me) a tad." She has, she said, been used to growing melons under glass, where hand-pollinating is a must. She concedes, however, that a melon plant out in the open is probably safely left to the bees. She added that at least it would give the neighbours a chuckle.

Like they need any help.

Notwithstanding that, the female flowers that I have indecently assaulted at her behest have definitely all set and are swelling nicely. I am in fact very proud of these – although I have become aware that I really must refrain from asking visitors if they would like to see my melons, as it does seem to elicit unwelcome responses.

My stated intention has always been to grow our crops here organically – that is, using our own composted material with no addition of chemical fertilisers and absolutely no anti-pest sprays. I am, to this end, following the "patchwork" planting method, where crops are all intersown to utterly confuse the pests.

"Look, there's a cabbage".

"No, no, you prat, look, it's a strawberry – that's no good to us."

"Strawberry? Prat yourself, it's got a big green melon-type fruit hanging from it."

"Well, it's not a cabbage, then, is it?"

"I'm sure I spotted a cabbage... oh, well, never mind – let's go next door and eat that neat row of lettuces."

This seems to have been working very well thus far – all of the plants are very prolific, and their produce healthy and, I have to say without modesty, delicious. Truly organic (unless, of course, you count Marcos peeing on them – that's one pest that isn't deterred by mixed planting!)

All entirely ruined yesterday, then, when our town-ward neighbour, who owns a huge plantation of peach trees two fields behind the barn, got out his own dis-tractor, hooked up a large white tank with more holes in it than a tea-bag and set off around his crops pumping out a fine mist of insecticide.

Fortunately, the parrots were all tucked safely away in the barn, because his chemicals managed to cover everything outside – my vegetables, the dogs, my washing, my car, me (ok, possibly no more spider bites, then, but that's not the point.)

So what I want to know is this – if you trot along to emporio Sainsbury and buy (ridiculously-inflated) genuine guaranteed organic produce, then how is it guaranteed? Is it grown in a bubble? Or does it have to be a certain distance away from cavalier neighbours who are happy to squirt their pollutants into the atmosphere and have the fall-out land on whatsoever and whomsoever it pleases?

Yours, etc. – Disgruntled of Bullas.

Having reached (by the skin of his teeth) the grand old age of three months, Marcos went off to see Alfonso the vet yesterday for his second batch of vaccinations. Even Alfonso was surprised at his size, and had to concede that, yes, he could well achieve full mastín proportions (as the examination table buckled under him…)

So I kept my promise to the postmaster and called in with Marcos to see him on the way home.

After a classic double-take and an ¡hombre! or two, he abandoned the exceedingly busy post office counter to come out and make a fuss of the excited puppy.

"Será muy grande," I said (accusingly).

"Sí," he replied, "Es porque yo soy tan alto" (It's because I am so tall).

This was met with, "Claro, claro" and much nodding of heads from all the patiently-waiting customers, while I was obliged to bite my lip hard and refrain from making the rejoinder that naturally sprang to mind. I'm still not sure enough of the Spanish sense of humour to ask, "¿Pues… por qué – eres su padre?" (Why? Are you then his father?)

Joggers

The camino that brings us from town to our finca continues weaving onwards through our land, from the point of entry next to Pedro and Loli's, down past the rooftop of the house on the right, across following the lower line of the barn area, then twisting back and forward upon itself as it descends through the various terraces to the river below, deteriorating in quality all the while, if that's possible.

At the bottom, there is a little stone bridge across the river, about eight foot in length, wide enough to allow passage on foot across the water.

The route, dropping now to the category of "sendero" (footpath) rather than "camino", then climbs steeply up again in almost a straight line on the other side of the valley. About half-way up, there is a turning to the right, about level with the barn terrace and caravan, that leads into a bridleway, used regularly by groups of riders from the local Centro Hípico, if they can find room amongst the hikers and joggers. It provides a very pleasant and shady walk, passing through pine trees but keeping sight of the river pretty much the whole time, and leading after about a half kilometre upstream to the local beauty spot known as El Salto de Usero.

El Salto means "The Jump", and legend has it that it was named for Usero the donkey, who fell to his death trying to jump across a chasm that opened up in a fault in the rock during a storm.

True or not, the chasm remains, spanned now by a picturesque wooden footbridge – on one side of the bridge, a small waterfall cascades as the river bed suddenly drops some thirty foot into a large bowl, seen opening up on the other side of the bridge. A pool of clear and cool water within the bowl is shaded by its sheer rock sides and by the hanging greenery clinging to the walls wherever it has found a foothold.

Bulleros have free and unimpeded access to this spot – it is affectionately known locally as "Costa de Bullas" – and as the weather warms up, it is normal to find at least half a dozen people cooling off in the water, or diving from the top of the waterfall into the deep water below it. During high days and holidays it is not unusual to find dozens of families perched around on ledges within the bowl, sat on towels and kindling portable barbecues.

Its whole charm lies in the total lack of any sign of commercialism – no bar, no ice-cream van, no entrance fees, and definitely no Africans selling watches – so refreshing.

From El Salto, a lane runs northwards back to the town; alternatively, there is a somewhat overgrown camino running off to the right that closes the circle back to a point just above our finca entrance.

I love this walk and, probably rather tediously, tend to drag visitors through it whenever possible. The only time I have ever done it and regretted it was the first time Marcos came with Donna and I, since having gambolled and rolled excitedly all the way down to the river, he decided that he was under no circumstances prepared to climb uphill on the other side. I therefore ended up carrying him for much of the way, and it disintegrated into the kind of aerobic-cum-weight-lifting exercise that I would normally avoid like the plague.

Talking of exercise, the beautiful La Rafa centre, situated at the townward end of our camino, boasts a large gym and fitness centre, running track, tennis courts, football pitch, huge lido and so on – and hosts a local jogging club, amongst other things.

The joggers love the circular route through our land and on to El Salto, and on a Thursday evening it is not unusual to witness the passage of a veritable gaggle of joggers. I've tried and failed to find a collective noun for joggers, so I've tried here the one for geese, although a "mustering" (of storks) would work quite well and I am also more than a little tempted by a "knob" (of pintails).

Last Thursday evening the normal knob of joggers (yeah, that's the one) thundered by. I admit that I have nothing but the greatest admiration for these people, in that they still manage to converse at the tops of their voices whilst jogging, where I would be struggling (and probably failing) just to breathe.

I was exercising on the terrace at the same time: I carried a heavy bottle of wine all the way from the barn to the table, and then managed a second circuit for the corkscrew and glass that I had forgotten first time. Exhausted, I sank into a chair to recover my breath and replace my vital liquid level.

Suddenly all hell broke loose below me.

A lone straggler had appeared around the bend. Qivi, already wound up by the passage of the knob, decided he wasn't allowing any more past, and streaked through our inadvertently-left-open barn gates barking dementedly and slavering profusely to confront this poor guy on the camino, effectively blocking his path. The jogger was yelling for help in terrified high-pitched squeaks and backing away from this rabid-looking wolf-beast, up to the point where the camino ran out and he was teetering on the edge of the drop to the next terrace down.

I had realised by then what had happened, and shouted sternly to Qivi to come back to heel. He looked up at me disgustedly, but (great wonders) decided to obey, slinking back with an occasional growl over his shoulder. I then spent five minutes apologising loudly across the distance to the quaking jogger, who had his right hand clutched to his left breast in a rather worrying fashion.

He managed to compose himself, though, after a short break, and jogged on. I settled back to my glass of wine.

The parrots were out enjoying the freshness of the evening air with me. Cookie was muttering away in cockatese, in his usual fashion, and Jack was pretending to be a fire engine, while Lucas sat quietly and observed us all wistfully, as a bird deeply in unrequited love tends to do.

As I gazed over the valley from my vantage point on the edge of the upper terrace, sipping my wine, it caught my eye that the poor jogger was making his way at walking pace back up the camino towards the barn. Hands on both hips and head down, looking depleted of energy and not a little dejected, I think the shock of a Qivi confrontation had completely broken his stride, and he had decided to head back to base with his tail between his legs.

I watched him toil laboriously back up the hill, feeling horribly guilty that Qivi had ruined his entire energetic evening.

Then, as he drew parallel with us on the camino below, Lucas suddenly decided to join the general parrot conversation, and let out a piercing wolf-whistle.

The jogger's head snapped up, and he met my eyes, glaring malevolently. From his viewpoint, stood below and looking up to the terrace, the parrots were not visible. I, frozen with wineglass raised half-way to my pursed-to-sip lips, could only stare back, unable to tear my eyes away and equally incapable of figuring out in that instant any way of denying my part in such an addition of insult to injury.

I wonder if he'll ever jog here again?

Face of a Town With No Teeth

Bullas is a town built on a mound, a feature it has in common with all of its immediate neighbours – Cehegín, Caravaca de la Cruz, Mula, Pliego and so on, all constructed in the fashion of a string of ant-hills along the ridges in this fairly mountainous area of North West Murcia.

One side of the hill invariably accommodates the old town, which is typically made up of rows and rows of very old terraced two- or three-storey houses face to face across steep and narrow cobbled lanes that can and do allow the passage of just one car at a time. The houses crowd directly onto the lanes, with no front yard and no pavement, and women in floral pinnies seem to spend much of their time deep in conversation across the gap from one first-floor balcony to another as they carry out their interminable cleaning duties.

It is not uncommon to find tables and chairs set up in (and subsequently blocking) the lanes themselves on a warm summer's evening, as cooking aromas and loud music emanate from open front doors. It's very quaint and somehow satisfyingly old-fashioned, and fills me with an enormous sense of well-being if I walk there.

It's a bugger, however, if on the other hand I accidentally stray into the labyrinth in my car. There have been occasions when I have entirely despaired of escaping its clutches.

The other side of the mound is usually much more modern and up-market, involving newer housing, shopping areas, recreation parks, medical facilities, restaurants and so on.

Then at the top (loosely speaking) are found the focal points of the town – all the pivotal buildings like the ayuntamiento offices and the main church, ranked proudly around the carefully-maintained and picturesque central plaza. Radiating from the central plaza, various roads and passageways lead off to smaller satellite plazas.

Our central plaza in Bullas boasts a large and ugly statue of a man looking for all the world like he's suffering from terminal constipation but is actually frozen for all time in the act of treading grapes. Not a flattering pose, it has to be said, but tremendously significant to Bullas in that it is a major wine-producer in the area, and arguably produces some of the finest wines in Spain (well, I'd argue it, anyway – and many restaurants, both here in Spain and back in the UK, are sufficiently in agreement to be putting Bullas wines firmly on their wine lists).

Strangely, the vine grows incredibly successfully in this very small area. I don't understand why – Mula, less than 20km east, grows citrus extensively, but we cannot do that here in Bullas. If I should want to grow a lemon tree here in order to pluck fresh lemons for the gin and tonic, then I would have to do so very carefully in a pot.

But we can produce grapes.

Just below the central plaza a small passageway runs alongside the main church (attractive enough in a utilitarian way from the outside; lofty, serious and awesome within) and descends to the modern shopping area via a small odd-shaped plaza. Here is to be found the indoor meat and fish market. This, it has to be said, is probably recognised as the university-standard training centre for queue-jumping. Open every weekday, it is the place to buy extremely fresh fish and good-quality meat (the latter not being my field, but I have it on excellent authority from the wildly-carnivorous Spanish).

Next door to the covered market there stands a community centre, aimed particularly at pensionistas. I have never yet been inside this building, but the door stands open most days and it is possible to see tables set out within, along with a bar area.

The pensionistas themselves eschew the interior comforts, however, preferring instead to gather in a large group outside the door on the small covered slightly-raised terrace area there, and to gossip and watch the entire world go by.

I have only ever seen old men there – in the same way that I only ever see groups of old men sat on the benches in the various tree-shaded recreation areas, taking the evening air. Either they must fly in the face of all statistics and outlive their women here, or, more likely, the women actually prefer to do their gossiping and people-watching from their first-floor balconies, cleaning all the while.

Anyway, I have to confess that I find it rather daunting to pass the community centre.

Since I am so obviously foreign, being blonde and fair-skinned, I appear to offend the natural order of things – and my passage will always elicit either the kind of embarrassed silence reserved for hideous mutations, or various mutterings about my unsuitable attire (I never wear enough in winter, apparently).

I feel that I really should, but doubt that I ever could, take the time to engage in conversation with these men – they must have a wealth of colourful stories to tell, including many, I suspect, of fighting as boy soldiers in the Spanish civil war. But the normal difficulties of Murcian Spanish descend into utter incomprehensibility in the mouths of the pensionistas – I've tried very hard to listen clandestinely to their interchanges and have so far drawn a total blank. I couldn't if pressed even be totally sure that they are in fact speaking Spanish.

And it is, of course, made much worse by the fact that twenty old men, all pretty healthy looking, and probably far fitter than me, what with all that walking up and down the lanes in the old town, between them are the proud owners of just three teeth. Big, brown, horsey and strong teeth, granted, and liberally bathed in continuous streams of spittle, but nonetheless, just the three.

That'll be a lifetime of churros and chocolate, then.

I think I'll stick to the healthy red wine option.

Midsummer & More Animal Madness

I made my habitual trip to Alicante airport on Saturday evening to collect John for his four days of work here between his rest periods in the UK. The flight was a little later than usual, and delays with baggage and traffic resulted in our arrival back here at the finca at gone eleven at night.

Normally, at this time of night, the whole valley would be swallowed in inky blackness, as the lights that John has kindly mounted on the front of the barn for me are switched off by a timeswitch at eleven.

But when we drove along the camino, just as we reached the valley edge and the point at which we start the descent onto our land, we could see soft lights playing on the pine trees on the other side of the valley.

"How strange," I said to John, "I wonder what that could be?"

"Something's going on at El Salto," he replied. "Take a look to your right."

There, on the bridle path across the river, almost at the point where the valley veers to the right to El Salto and passes out of our sight from the terrace, we could see dozens of lights bobbing madly up and down like hyperactive fireflies.

71

A procession of people carrying flaming torches was making its way steadily towards the waterfall and bowl.

I've never taken an awful lot of notice of summer solstice, apart from some hazy awareness that there was possibly still in existence in the UK a group of people that might make their way to Stonehenge or other such weirding sites at the appropriate time in order to sacrifice a virgin or two, and that, possibly because they couldn't face the paperwork it would involve, the police did their utmost to stop them. But even in my ignorance of such things, I worked out that this was probably a midsummer thing.

Then, at midnight, just as John was heaving his case out of the car boot, suddenly the still strings of the night air were strummed by some invisible hand and a deep and sonorous chord rang out, filling the whole valley.

The music, played half a kilometre away through some exceedingly good equipment and in a natural sound chamber, was loud, pure and clear, a sort of primal earth music, and I simply can't find any better word to describe it than "magical".

We succumbed immediately – grabbing the bottle of wine I had previously opened to breathe, and a couple of glasses, we dived top-to-tail on the double hammock under the fig tree, and allowed ourselves to be washed for an hour by the beautiful sounds as we swayed gently, watching the stars and sipping our wine, agreeing humbly that this was one of life's quietly awesome moments.

Next year I want to be there.

Marcos, whom I admit to having mis-named, since in retrospect I should clearly have called him Shrek, has been toad-hunting. As we live in a river valley, there are obviously a lot of toads around, although we don't see them in the normal course of events because they are largely nocturnal. We do hear them loud and clear at night, especially the rasping gargle of the natterjack toad (bufo calamita) as it calls at both length and volume for a mate. Largely unsuccessfully, it would seem.

Anyway, Marcos suddenly appeared from the lower slopes on Sunday with a huge toad in his mouth.

I cannot stand animal cruelty of any kind, even if inflicted by one non-human animal upon another. I'm still carefully rescuing spiders and placing them gently away from the caravan, despite my spider love-bite. And much to the annoyance of most of our friends, I won't countenance the killing even of flies and wasps in my company. So the sight of this poor creature firmly wedged in Marcos' cakehole caused me some consternation.

I grabbed a pair of gloves and rugby-tackled Marcos to the floor, prized open his jaws, and extracted … an empty toad.

This poor thing was long-dead. It was the remains of a common toad (bufo bufo – all right, so I looked these up; I didn't know them before, OK?), some six inches long, and looking and feeling for all the world like a perfect papier-mâché model of a toad.

Now while this was going on, John and Pedro were leaning on the digger, deep in gesticulation (they don't do conversation, remember) about the necessity of replacing the old hydraulic oil for the rams to function better. You really don't want a graphical description of this interchange, trust me.

So I approach them to show them the empty sapo.

Pedro looks up, spots the toad, shrieks and skips backwards in a real girly fashion, pulls a lemon-sucking face and mimes the toad squirting something extremely smelly out of its back end (another one you wouldn't wish me to describe fully, in all honesty).

I had to laugh, such was his consternation, and I rattled the husk of the poor thing and then drop-kicked it away.

Pedro, realising that he probably looked pretty silly, turned upon me angrily to save face, and sternly waggled an admonishing finger at me.

"You," he said, "Refuse to see the dangers here. First you ignore my warnings about the spiders," (gesturing at my leg), "and then you go playing with toads. I can see that I will end up taking you to Caravaca to the hospital."

"Or worse," he added ominously, for extra effect.

I am suitably chastened.

Meanwhile, Marcos has seen his latest toy thrown for his pleasure, and fetches it back.

And wherever I secrete it away now to disintegrate back into the soil with dignity, Marcos finds it. It currently has pride of place sat in the middle of the terrace, like some gothic gnome.

The other monster in my menagerie, Cookie, caused further uproar recently. He, also misnamed, should have been Houdini, without a shadow of a doubt. He doesn't want to escape from us, he wants to come to find us, as he is a classic cockatoo and would be more than happy to be skin-grafted to one of us. But he gets sidetracked by all manner of interesting distractions en route.

So I entered the parrot room to find the side door into the long barn, previously locked shut, swinging open. A quick glance showed me that the key to this door, minus its coloured plastic jacket, was lying in the bottom of Cookie's cage. Not one to stay on his cage when there's important exploring to be done, Cookie had descended to the floor and hop-skipped into the long barn.

My washing machine, tumble dryer and ironing board are all set up in this barn – and what better climbing frame can there be than an ironing board?

Sherpa Cookie was sat proudly on top of my big steam generator iron – which was by this time in kit-form.

All the control knobs and switches were strewn around him like Christmas wrapping paper, the cover plate from the top of the handle had been prised off, and all the wires that regulate the steam function were chewed down to the last millimetre.

Completely unrepairable, then. And of course I'm in deep trouble for letting him (get through a locked door…)

But John had to eat his words the very next day.

He had taken Cookie out of his cage in the cool of the early morning and walked around with him on his shoulder while watering the vegetable plot and pottering about generally. Then he perched him on a branch in the fig tree while he came back into the caravan to grab his coffee.

Cookie loves the fig tree – he can climb about to his heart's content, completely hidden from the sight of potential predators above. The only problem is that he can only be left for about five minutes because otherwise he would strip off all the leaves and figs and bark and it wouldn't be much of a fig tree then.

So John is on his way back out with his coffee, and I glance out as he goes, only to spot a flash of white on the electricity pylon.

Cookie has descended from the fig tree in double time (this is all walking and climbing, by the way – he rarely flies, although he can), has hopped across the five metre gap to the umbrella, which is braced from the pylon against the wind, and thence onto the pylon itself.

And he is climbing fast.

I shouted to John, who hadn't taken this in yet, and dashed over to the base of the pylon to try to coax Cookie down.

Cookie wanted to come back – he kept craning down looking for a way to reach back to the next lower rung – but clearly found it too daunting and so continued upwards, which was far easier.

So John raced over to the pylon, leapt at it in true fireman fashion, and proceeded to shin up too.

Cookie, realising that all this was going to end in him being grounded, obviously decided to make the most of it and climbed faster. By the time John reached him, they were both about seven metres off the ground and less than three metres from the overhead cables that carry the entire supply of electricity across the valley.

Meanwhile, Pedro and his family, having heard the commotion (and anyway being generally exceedingly nosey and probably knowing far more of our goings-on than we realise) were ranged along the fence whistling and cheering words of encouragement – whether to John or Cookie, I couldn't in all honesty be sure.

They must bless the day we appeared here with all our wordly goods to share this little corner of the campo with them. We're so much more entertaining than Spanish television...

THE "SARDINE TIN"

OLD BULLAS

REFORMED CASITA

SMOKEY

ASH

JADE, QIVI AND MARCOS

J.T.

LUCAS

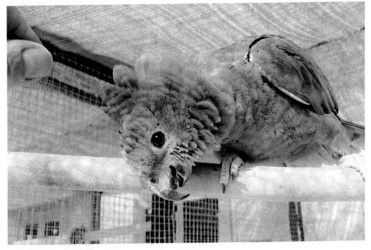

COOKIE

SWEETPEA

PICKLE

JACK

NOODLE

SKETCH OF MURCIA REGION

Overheating &
Camomile Tea

I know, I made a solemn promise that if we could just sell the villa I'd be a good girl and live a quiet and uncomplaining existence in the caravan for as long as it takes to get the house done properly.

And I am trying very hard to behave, to be resigned to the myriad difficulties and discomforts that this obviously throws up.

I've dealt with electricity cuts, I've gone without water for a couple of days at a time, I take my rubbish on sight-seeing tours, I clean dust off the car umpteen times a week, I walk kilometres back and forth between the caravan and the barn to produce a meal and to feed the zoo. I empty loose gravel and campo debris out of my shoes a zillion times every day. And so on.

But nobody warned me just how ridiculously hot a caravan can get. When it is 35°C in the shade outside, it hits well over 40°C inside the caravan.

Forgive me for being naïve, but aren't these things rented out en masse by large and prosperous companies to happy holidaymakers for fun in the sun? What sort of sadists are these people?

Another issue bothering me greatly and that had never even crossed my mind beforehand is the fact that I am never, ever able to get cold water. The caravan is linked to the mains by a waterpipe running overground with minimal cover, and the solar gain it suffers is tremendous. While it proves the point that we will have no trouble in obtaining an abundance of free hot water in the house, that is small consolation when I can't even run off a bowl of cold water for the dogs to drink. And as for the shower – well, I have made the fatal error a couple of times now of forgetting to reduce the boiler temperature in readiness for a shower. So when I get in, and it's a little warm, I automatically and moronically turn on the cold tap in a vain attempt to cool it down. Instead, it gets even hotter, and I find myself plastered against the door desperately trying to avoid the scorching deluge, watching my skin slough off in layers.

I'm really not capable of dealing with high temperatures. I love to see blue skies and sun – but in the heat of the day I like to be well out of it somewhere cool. And yes, that is a truly Spanish perspective. The Spanish will all be firmly tucked away indoors busy at their siesta during the sizzling afternoons – it's only the Northern Europeans you will see morphing through the various shades of pink to black stretched out in full sun on the beach.

Up here on the terrace, there is very little escape from the heat. The three large and leafy fig trees do give some shade, but at this time of year the sun is pretty much directly overhead, and anyway, there's never any room for me amongst the prone bodies of panting dogs. If there's a breeze blowing then it affords a little respite; if not, outside is definitely not the place for me.

But inside a caravan is unbearable.

And if I overheat, I get psychotically, axe-murderously bad-tempered, as John would willingly vouch.

As a result, more I suspect in a gesture of self-preservation than anything else, John suggested that we have a small air-conditioning unit installed in the lounge area of the caravan. So after all the usual discussions about unbudgeted expenditure, short-term problems and so on, we came to the spurious conclusion that if we really wanted our family and friends to visit us in future and use the caravan (we don't, after all, want them in the house with us, do we?) then it would be much more comfortable for them too if it had air-conditioning.

As I write this, therefore, there is cool air playing over my head and shoulders and I feel human again …at least, as human as possible for arachnid woman.

My spider bite is still looking angry and unhealed, some eight weeks now after the event. I stopped going to the clinic a couple of weeks ago, for two reasons – the first was that I had spent some time researching spider bites on the internet, and found that all websites I visited without fail recommended that the wound should never be cut, since it is likely to cause further tissue necrosis; and that oral antibiotics were a waste of time. This caused me to suffer a rapid loss of faith in their methods at the clinic, strongly supported by the fact that the thing was clearly not responding to their ministrations. Secondly, the numbers of walking wounded seeking attention at the clinic each time I went (every other day) was rising exponentially, as was therefore the time I spent sat there awaiting my turn.

Anyhow, I decided to call it a day.

Two weeks on, then, although it still hasn't changed much, at least it's not being lanced and smothered any more, and actually feels better in that it itches quite a lot (which our paternal grandmother always held to mean that it's healing).

However, as Pedro misses no opportunity to tell me, it is "feo" (ugly). And I know for sure that he means the wound, because if he was calling me ugly it would, of course, be "fea".

And he would, of course, be "muerto" (dead).

So today I went and saw a private Doctor in Caravaca de la Cruz, whose instructions were to leave it uncovered to dry where possible (sensible), to clean it with saline solution (sensible), and to apply to it three times a day a cold compress... soaked in chilled camomile tea (*whaaat?*)

I paid for this advice? I give up.

While I was out, I also had cause to invest in some large dustbins with lockable lids. This is a result of a certain puppy and a recent infatuation of his with ripping open any plastic bag he should encounter in pursuit of the chance that it may just contain some small scraps of food waste.

He will eat anything. Broccoli stalks, bird seed husks, an empty tuna can and tissues were on his midnight snack menu last night. Rounded off with a couple more bites out of the shell of the hapless toad, which now resembles a scrunch-dried Chamois leather.

He has also managed to destroy two plastic water bowls, has irretrievably hidden my broom, dustpan and mop somewhere in the tall undergrowth below us, and has recently started again on the vegetable patch.

I'm seriously thinking of posting him back to the Correos without a return address.

I must include just one more short and certainly rather tasteless note about little Marcos (that's affectionate, rather than descriptive, by the way).

He's now about fifteen weeks old and weighs in at eighteen kilos. He eats more in fun than two pigs in earnest, but there's not a bit of fat on him, because he is as perpetually in motion as a box of frogs.

He spends half his time these days diving about in the long grasses on the lower slope of this terrace, which results in his fur being constantly full of burrs.

I have just, therefore, taken the dog comb to him in a vain attempt to remove all the offending articles and to tease out some of the knots.

I expected this exercise to be a full-blown fight to keep him still enough to comb without taking out an eye (his or mine, either way). But on the contrary – he obviously enjoyed it greatly.

So greatly, in fact, that for the first time in his life (to my knowledge) he got out his dog pinkie.

Good grief! You know what they say about size of feet...

Neighbours: Good & Bad

We have here in the finca some wonderful neighbours in the shape of la familia Pedro next door – when they are in residence, we share incessant banter over the fence, and mucho vino o cafe on one terrace or another. When things break or fail for us, Pedro is only too willing to step into the breach with a solution, and when we are feeling low about progress here (or the lack thereof) he plays the clown to lift our spirits. Loli is always on hand with sustenance and a quiet calm. We couldn't wish for better vecinos, albeit part-time.

On the other hand, we have a neighbour to our north-east who is, not to put too fine a point on it, un cabrón.

His house is some three hundred metres behind and to the left of our barn, almost (but not quite) hidden from view by his almond groves. And apparently his is the most disliked family in the whole of Bullas. All his neighbours hate him, as he has, at some stage or other in his career, screwed over each and every one of them. He reneged on payment to the old lady who previously owned our property after the electricity lines were brought in, despite the fact that it was supposed to be a joint cost and he still has the use of the lines, carried on a post further down our land. Apparently he has recently played the same trick on his neighbour on the other side of his house, having agreed to share the cost of works to their dedicated camino and then refusing to cough up.

When we first bought the land here, long before we actually moved across, he challenged us through the small length of back fence at the right-hand end of the barn.

"You have no right to this," he stated. "The barn is built on my land – and my daughter is a lawyer, so we will fight you for it."

Oh, good grief! So we spoke immediately to Jose, who sold it to us in the first place, and who, after piling a whole heap of invective and doubt upon the parentage of said neighbour, suggested that we employ a topógrafo (surveyor) to clarify that our copy of the catastro (property register) was correct.

This we did, at the cost of 500€, merely to ascertain that we were fine and all was correct – the old man had no claim upon our barn.

However, he did say to Jose that we must not reform the barn, as we had originally intended, since it is right on his boundary, and he would object loudly. Well, actually, that is not entirely true – he said we could reform it, but only if we paid him 9,000€ hush-money to keep his mouth shut.

Jose, high and rising by this time, told him that we would not even pay him 9,000 mierdas (look it up).

But because of this situation, and not wishing to appear in any way confrontational, we did decide to turn our attentions to the old casita lower down, rather than the barn.

Unlike the barn, the house did not show up on the catastro. Primarily, therefore, we would need to have its existence and antiquity verified officially.

The old house was small and dilapidated, perched on a terrace two levels below the barn, more private than the barn itself, and, in fact, with even better views. It bore a corrugated roof atop worm-ridden wooden beams, and single-skin walls. The floor levels inside were bizarre, to say the least, and the windows, still barred, were tiny. It boasted a kitchen-cum-lounge with a big built-in corner fire and old pot Belfast-style sink, and three small bedrooms, all leading one from the other. The toilet stood (still stands) in a brick-built cupboard with no door about seventy-five metres away from the house.

We spoke to a firm of builders that had been quite active in Sucina during our residence there, to look at plans for reforming and extending this property. An architect was brought in and duly charged us 1,500€ for measuring it and preparing the necessary papers for its registration. He was also to apply for the building licence to reform and extend it. He approved my designs for a simple, rustic, single-storey two-bedroomed structure, which he took away to re-state professionally on his CAD system for submission.

Four months later, in April 2006, we were informed by the builder that everything was in place and that he would be starting on site the following week. John was unfortunately in the UK, but I made the journey from Sucina to Bullas every day for two weeks to watch the removal of all parts of the old house too dilapidated to save, and the amazing phoenix-like growth of the new house.

Five weeks later, the extended building was fully up as a box to roof level, and was ready to receive its hat.

Then, one fine day in June 2006, the inspector of works from the ayuntamiento visited the site. I was not there at the time, but I drove over the very next day – to find that the site was completely deserted. The builders had disappeared, taking all their tools, scaffolding, mixers, everything. There were not even any surplus building materials lying around outside, although there were some bags of cement and various assorted bits of masonry shoved inside the house.

I tried to phone the builder, only to find that the number was no longer available. I even drove over to his office address, shown on our original quote (the only paperwork I have to show for our liaison), but, lo and behold, it doesn't exist.

We had paid fairly and squarely for the work completed at that point – we have no problems on that score. However, I then received a letter from the ayuntamiento saying that we were building without a licence and must cease immediately.

Spilt milk and all that – we realise, in hindsight, that we should have demanded to see the paperwork that the builder and his architect were supposed to have sent and received. But we were remote, naïve, and above all, trusting. Silly us.

Jose discovered that the ayuntamiento had been alerted to the building works within one week of their commencement when our dear sweet black-mailing neighbour went to them and denounced us, having enquired about our licence to build and discovered that there had been no application for one.

Jose and Nathalie were absolutely wonderful. They arranged meetings with the mayor, at which I was able to state that we had been misled by builders and to present our plans anew. The mayor was actually very supportive – I said that my future plans were to place picnic tables and shades on the land for walkers to use, to encourage people to visit this beautiful spot, and that I hoped that my rescued parrots would prove to be an additional attraction for families. He nodded encouragingly through most of this and promised to help us in every way that he could. The house would stand, he said, and we would live in it soon, but obviously we would have to pay a fine first since things had not been conducted in the correct manner.

So we waited interminably for the fine.

The mayor promised that the fine would be evaluated "next week"… "in fifteen days"… "next month"… but nothing materialised. Exasperated, Jose went to see the mayor the following February, to be told that there was such a backlog of cases that the fine would not be produced until September.

"Don't worry," the Mayor said, "Tell your clients to finish the structure. I will look the other way."

And he has – so we have been able to finish the roof, put in the windows and internal walls, and render and decorate with stone the outside walls. This was finished mid-May.

Local elections took place throughout Spain in June 2007. Our previous mayor's party managed to scrape back into office by the skin of its teeth and by sneakily amalgamating with the Izquierda – the left party - but our friendly mayor, although still working within the party, made way for another. The new mayor has not yet been available for any appointments whatsoever – apparently he is still working as a teacher in Murcia and is not around much. He does have a new Concejal, though. This is the guy that moves paperwork around within the ayuntamiento and sends out letters.

The new Concejal is, we have discovered, related to el cabrón behind us. He didn't even give decent pause, following the elections, before sending us a letter saying that we had disobeyed previous orders by roofing the house and finishing the exterior, and that the house would now be sealed by the Policía Local. We think he even had the letter ready before-hand to slide under the mayor's careless pen at the first opportunity.

Oh jolly good. And that leaves us… where?

Jose wants to kill someone. He wants equity – there are three thousand houses built without licence in the Bullas area and not one has been treated like this before. It would very much seem that we are the victims now of a vendetta.

All is not lost, however. We may yet have something en las mangas – and this is the real kicker. John happened to be checking out the depuradora recently at the eastern-most edge of this top terrace, when he spied workmen through the trees on the roof of el cabrón's house in the distance, clearly undertaking building work. So on Friday last he and Jose went undercover, sneaking around in the undergrowth on this guy's land with a camera, and giggling like two naughty schoolboys, primarily with nerves and then with sheer elation to see and to photograph a brand-new two-storey house that he is building alongside his own without permission!

Watch this space…

Summer Life

Pedro's cockerel next door has now graduated and is all grown up. The father of four adorable little chicks, he no longer feels it acceptable to take for himself, nor allow for others, the luxury of rising later than six o'clock in the morning.

Any attempt I may make to bury my head in my pillow and to steal just a little more time swimming in the pool of semi-conscious laziness is in vain. As far as the dogs are concerned, the cock crow appears to correspond to a referee's whistle and their signal to kick off their early morning daily game of football.

Well, it's something a lot like football, anyway, in that it incontrovertibly involves much running around with and a whole lot of arguing about a ball.

So I am left little choice but to give in and get up.

Throwing the caravan door wide to a new day, I am at least able at that time of the morning to enjoy a brief window of cool and pleasant air, where an hour later I know that I will be transformed into a limp and melting waxwork by the blast furnace outside. I am, however, already blinded by the ferocious sunlight, so that I am utterly incapable of sight when I step out into dog soup.

Wading through the excited hounds, who haven't seen me for, what? seven hours?, I search for their water bowls, fish out any creatures still alive therein and then refresh them while breakfast is cooking for the parrots.

Then into the barn to open the blinds, and to give the stretching and yawning feathered goblins their wholewheat rice and fruit and vegetables so they can tuck in while I change their water and clean the bottoms of the cages.

A quick watering of the vegetable plot and potted plants before it gets too hot, and only then am I free to indulge myself with a shower.

I fire up the computer to see if anyone out there has bothered to recall my existence, and then I can settle down to the first critical morning caffeine fix. Oh, and now I have to brew for my leg the first of its thrice-daily cups of camomile tea.

I feel like a hedge witch.

You can tell it's July and blisteringly hot here now. All the previously-lush greens have faded to a sort of mucky khaki colour, and the ground is baked rock-hard. Every gust of wind raises clouds of thick dust, creating a hazy, shimmery and unmistakably hot, dry overlay of the landscape. The vegetables are all listless and unhappy, and even the trees look cowed. The only flowers in bloom are irises, hibiscus and dipladenia, all in hellish blood-red, seemingly to emphasise the heat. The cigarras have taken out their buzz-saws and are busy carving up the countryside in their desperate bid to mate before they die. The awful continuous high-pitched ear-rending whine that they produce throughout the hot season is enough to fry totally a brain that is already stupefied by the heat, and it seems as if there must be a whole swarm of the ruddy things sat in the nearest tree competing for the decibel output annual cup. But when it stops abruptly, it becomes apparent that it was actually just the one lone performer managing single-handedly to fill the universe with its jaw-aching racket. I only hope potential mates find the noise more attractive than I do.

I'm told that they are edible, and although they emit a noise exactly like they are made entirely of metal parts, and certainly don't sound even vaguely appetising, the cat seems to rate them quite highly. Marcos probably eats them, too – he eats everything else.

The garden fairies have called, by the way, and turned all my melons into pumpkins. And I am not referring here to melons the size of pumpkins, either. I have been misled over and over again about this surprise element of my vegetable patch, what with duff advice about pollination and so forth. So when I picked one this morning that appeared to be splitting, and took a knife to slice it, I couldn't understand why a melon, normally of soft flesh and fairly easily-cut skin, should sit there so unyielding as to turn the knife aside and almost through my own hand. This became easily comprehensible, however, when I realised that it was in fact no melon but a gourd of sterner stuff.

So we were looking forward to devouring our own juicy fresh melons and have instead half a dozen pumpkins to digest. Somehow, I just don't think it'll be the same.

I was caught in the midst of another undesirable summer phenomenon on Friday. Having dropped our breadwinner off at Alicante airport following his David Bailey impersonations next door with Jose, and after a clear and free run to get there, I turned the car around and pointed it in the direction of home. For me, from Alicante, this involves driving south-west and then more-or-less due west. At around eight in the evening, this of course means that I am driving into the sun most of the time, which is a gloriously beautiful but somewhat dangerous experience. As the sun dips lower and gets redder, tingeing the tops of all the distant mountain ridges with pinks as the halo of the sky darkens, I am obliged to squint more and more. Sunglasses and sun visors are mere trifles against the assault of the glaring rays of a low sun. I also admit to driving too fast, as I race the sun to arrive back before it finally sinks below the horizon and draws up its black sheets for sleep, leaving the valley dark and uninviting for my return home alone.

This time, though, on a fine July Friday evening, driving too fast was completely out of the question. The whole E15 between the airport junction and Murcia was grinding painfully along like an elderly tortoise using a zimmer frame.

An accident? Roadworks? A demonstration by disgruntled lorry-drivers? None of these more obvious things. And certainly not the incessant rain and rising rivers currently paralysing the roads of Britain, either.

Sheer weight of traffic had brought the flow to a ponderous standstill. And then, inching tortuously forward, with all the car windows down and my music on, gazing in disbelief at the vast numbers of cars stretching endlessly away in front of me and noting the same echoed in my rear view mirror, it suddenly struck me that they were all "foreign"! I was entirely surrounded by hundreds upon hundreds of cars all bearing the "NL" membership badge, all in convoy, all passing sandwiches, crisps, sweets and drinks back and forth between vehicles.

Clearly, then, the Dutch schools had just broken up for the summer vacation and in response to this the entire Dutch community had packed all its worldly goods and relations into SUVs and was hurling itself like a pack of lemmings at Spain.

Pity, I thought, as a young girl from the car in front of me tottered past my car bearing a large box of sliced chocolate cake for the inhabitants of the car behind me, that I can't speak Dutch...

Memories & Frustrations

I have been transported back to my childhood. Memories surface of happy and carefree days when it was still fine to spend long summer days messing around at the water's edge in an old disused and flooded quarry, fishing for all manner of pondlife and making dens in the thickly tangled greenery crowding its edge. Boys and tomboys together, all getting dirty and wet, out of sight in a private world if not out of mind.

Of course, that was in the days before the "Fear of Everything" culture overtook Britain, and when politicians hadn't yet reached the stage of this burning need for total control over every daily activity.

But I digress. The reason that I felt as though I was nine years old again (in mind if certainly not in body) was that the river was calling for assistance.

The bridge across the river at the bottom of the camino is built directly onto the riverbed across its entire width, there being no piers; but it does have small pipes set laterally into the stonework below the water which allow the passage of the river through what would otherwise be a solid wall.

We noticed recently, whilst ambling about with the dogs at the bottom of the land, that the river was growing wider and shallower as it was finding its way around rather than through the bridge. Apart from making it much harder to cross, since there was now a widening stretch of unspanned water either side of the bridge itself, it was also making something of a mess with the erosion of the sendero in both directions. The channels through the stones had obviously become blocked with all manner of floating debris washed to the bridge from upstream.

So there we were, two full-grown adults, laying face-down across the bridge with sticks, poking around under the water amongst the fish and the myriad of other water creatures I had long forgotten, like water boatmen and pond skaters, trying to locate the holes through the structure below us.

The jet-black dragonflies hovered nervously around us, unsure of the intentions of these large and strange creatures rolling about childishly on the bridge, but aware that we could well be stirring up some lunch. And, just as it was when we were kids, we were, between the dogs and ourselves, churning so much mud from the bottom that we couldn't see a blind thing. Even when we eventually managed to locate the holes, we broke the long thin sticks we were trying to use, and made the problem worse. Eventually John heroically trotted off all the way back up to the barn to get a couple of iron rods so that we could do the job properly.

We were then, with enough twisting and tamping, able to force through the leaves, bits of stick and other jammed objects that were impeding the water's progress, and were delighted to see the river once again pushing through the proper channels to emerge in a swirling cloud downstream of the bridge, while the outlying trespassing pools receded slowly back to flow once again within their rightful boundaries.

I think we may have just volunteered for a job for life.

I spent a typical day in Spain today – wasting a lot of time achieving absolutely zero whilst having stacks to do.

I had an appointment at 10:30 this morning to meet Jose at his office and thence to go to talk to the mayor at the ayuntamiento offices in the main plaza.

Amazingly, Jose was actually there when I arrived. This could be an all-time first, certainly in my memory - but then I had to sit and wait for half an hour for him to finish a phone call, make another, and then to talk to a friend that had happened to pop in to see him. We finally made the town hall at around 11:10, to be told that the mayor was at his almuerzo until 11:30.

No problem – Jose decided that we too would go to the bar, to see if we could perhaps spot the great man himself and conduct our meeting in the bar – a far more civilised place in which to discuss all matters of import in any case, as any Spaniard will affirm.

So we proceeded to the bar on the plaza, where regrettably the mayor was not available to deal concurrently with my problems and a plate of sardinas, as someone else had clearly nobbled him first.

So Jose had a small snack – two panecillos, a beer and a coffee, while I settled for a cortado (short strong coffee), and suffered the usual stigma of being the only woman, and a strange-looking one at that, in an all-male enclave. I suppose I should be used to it all by now – one, the fact that I am clearly not a native of Spain and therefore attract all sorts of unwanted attention, and two, that the attention is so openly child-like and unashamed. Catch an Englishman staring at you and he will jump through hoops to make out that he was trying to see something beyond you to excuse himself for having been caught with his eyes astray somewhere on your anatomy; catch a Spaniard, and he will carry on staring blatantly while it is you who feels obliged to look away and defuse the embarrassment (yours, never theirs).

Fortunately, the proprietor had his small grandson in the bar with him today, so I was able to ignore all the old lechers and occupy myself by playing peek-a-boo with him.

Shame he'll grow up to be an old letch too, really.

Having fortified himself, Jose decided that we would then go to the Oficina Técnica to speak to someone important there. Upon arriving, however, he was told that all of the officers that he would need to see were out and that he would have to return tomorrow at an appointed time.

So he then declared that we would go to the nearby bank to speak to one of the tellers there who just so happens to be the son-in-law of my dearest neighbour – why, I'm not quite sure, except that he showed me that his mobile phone was set up to record the conversation. Very Dick Tracy – unfortunately thwarted when he was told that his man was on holiday until next week.

Back to the town hall, then, to be told that the mayor is now in a meeting. It is by this time almost one o'clock and we have achieved precisely nothing.

Not quite nothing, actually. While we were in the town hall the second time, the Concejal who had sent me the last letter appeared, and Jose tackled him about the matter. He was very defensive and said that it was a difficult situation, but Jose replied that he trusted it would become much clearer tomorrow, and the guy looked somewhat hunted.

Jose has said to me that if this is not resolved equitably, then he will take it to the press and the television. Yeah, and I'm on the first plane back to the UK in that case, trust me.

If I wasn't actually personally caught up in it, I'd say it was part of an improbable and particularly poor soap opera anyway.

So we await the next episode...

Domesticity & Spanish Dinner Parties

Today I have had to dig up and level the entire vegetable patch. Standing as it did between the caravan and the edge of the terrace, it lay directly in the path between the tractor and the bund in which we have placed the depuradora, and we now need to move a large amount of soil to finish back-filling the bund.

Sadly, then, since for a trial run it has proved to be incredibly successful, I have stripped out all remaining fruits of my labours - carrots, shallots, courgettes, green tomatoes, pumpkins, parsley, mint and strawberries.

¿Melones? No (tut). No hay.

So my little green forest at the foot of the caravan steps is now nothing more than a flat brown rectangle.

Nothing will go to waste, of course. The mint, parsley and strawberries have all been replanted in pots. The carrots and courgettes will be consumed this evening with a nice piece of salmon fillet in orange sauce. The shallots are steeped in brine as I write, ready to pickle tomorrow. The green tomatoes are sat waiting to be chutneyfied. And I have spicy pumpkin soup (in the pumpkin - a French recipe á la Sue) simmering gently in the oven, and smelling, I must say, rather good, along with a tray of pumpkin seeds roasting for the parrots. Hey! Who needs shops?

Well, actually, I can't make decent bread to save my life and wine just takes far too long to keep up with demand...

I was invited to join Pedro and Loli for la cena last night, along with six more of their closest friends and drinking partners. So according to our custom I packed a carrier bag with essential items – a bottle of wine, a carrot cake, a shawl, a torch to see my way home; and I took off for next door at a time I deemed to be decent and appropriate by Spanish standards - around half-past nine.

I was the first to arrive, by almost an hour.

When the other guests did finally roll up, it was, to my surprise, empty-handed. This, then, would probably explain the confused looks I received from my hosts when I appeared with offerings for the table. And as you can probably guess, it also resulted in the return this morning of my cake tin full of fresh eggs, tomatoes and peaches.

Fortunately, my early arrival didn't hold up proceedings – there was nothing to do until all the guests had arrived, since dinner was to be made up of giant king prawns in the shell (cooked in the wood oven outside), along with olives and almonds to start, followed by a huge mixed barbecue, diced tomatoes and bread for the main course – all served with about twenty lemons. Not taxing on the kitchen in any way.

The table was, of course, laden with bottles, and I am endlessly amazed by the Spanish capacity to mix up drinks ferociously without any obvious ill effect. We started with copious amounts of beer, followed by equal amounts of red wine. Then with coffee came various assorted shots – crème de menthe, lemoncillo, coffee liqueur, crema de oruja (don't ask me – I can't abide creamy drinks) and of course, brandy. Then to round it all off, cava, of all things.

I admit that I struggled to keep up with the conversation. I normally manage fairly well with Pedro, and very well with Loli, who, dear soul, speaks deliberately slowly and clearly for me. But eight of them all gabbling at top speed, high volume and, more importantly, over each other, stretched me to the very limits.

Strange to say, though, I did understand all the many rude bits…

I was, however, placed in a difficult spot at one point. Having always called me Débora, Pedro recently heard John call me Debbie and has since taken delight in calling me débil (which means weak, feeble). So they had a bit of fun with that, until I pointed out to Alfonso that his diminutive Foli means "locura", or crazy act, in English. This of course started something – Loli, whose full title is Dolores, was tickled to find out that her diminutive in English means "piruleta" or lollipop.

Fine so far – and then I was asked by Estafanía about an English translation of her diminutive – Fani.

Oh, bugger.

They say that he who hesitates is lost. Had I been quicker, I could probably have got away with saying that there was no translation. But I paused for a nanosecond too long, and they were onto it like a pack of dogs with a bone.

"Is it worse than Foli?" they cried.

"Much worse," I replied, firmly.

"Tell us, tell us, tell us!"

Well, I'm nothing if not honest, so I told them, using the only word I know for it in Spanish – "coño" - a word, I must say in my defence, that I feel can't be as dreadful in Spanish as it would be in English, as I have even heard it fall with impunity from the lips of the most respectable-looking and well-turned-out of elderly Spanish ladies.

They howled. Paco, Fani's husband, ended up on the floor, unable to rise, such was his mirth. And I spent the rest of the evening apologising profusely to poor Fani.

More Mischief & Birthday Parties

Jose called me on my mobile a few days ago to proclaim excitedly that he has taken the photographs acquired clandestinely by him and John to the Oficina Técnica, and has denounced our spiteful neighbour for building without permission. He declared gleefully that the work on said neighbour's new house has therefore also been halted.

Half of me disapproves of this – I don't tend to be of the tit-for-tat persuasion, being much more likely to turn the other cheek in the hope that the situation will diffuse itself. However, the other half is delighted because he had it coming and maybe by standing up to him he can be persuaded to get out of our faces. And anyway, so far the turning of the other cheek has merely resulted in both sides being slapped instead of just the one.

However, a couple of days later we went down to our house to show some friends around the outside, having explained that we were unable to enter the house itself which was "precintada" (sealed), only to find it open. Someone had cut the wire sealing the front door, had found the door itself locked, and had subsequently broken in through a tilt-and-turn window at the front that I had left open for nesting birds and was subsequently unable to shut again having then been denied access.

So we unlocked the door and entered, to discover that the intruder had left a strange piece of vandalism as a calling card. The incoming mains electric cable had been totally severed at ground level, and the previously-attached fuse box lay discarded and smashed on the floor, with its circuit-breakers still in place. The toma de tierra, or earth wire, was also severed at ground level, and all cables had been removed, included the power lead to an old radio.

The French doors into the dining room stood open where the thief had made an exit.

There was absolutely no other damage done.

I am utterly confused as to how the intruder managed to cut right through a live mains wire without damaging himself or blowing my entire supply?

Now, it may be that I am being completely paranoid here, but I admit that my first thought was that this sort of wanton destruction had to be a further act of retaliation by Mr. Personailty next door. The only thing that such handiwork could possibly achieve was great inconvenience and some cost to us, since we now have no electricity in the house and we will have to bring in an electricista to fix it quite soon as it is clearly dangerous to have a cut but still live cable hanging around.

So off I trotted with Jose back to the Guardia Civil in order to make a denuncia myself – against an unknown person – and to log the fact that it wasn't us who broke the seal on the house, just in case the Policía Local should ever ask.

Pedro, uncannily aware that something was amiss, bellowed instructions to us to join them for a beer later that evening, this being his tried and tested method of putting the world to rights. Luisa had previously let me know that this was in fact Loli's birthday, so we were happy to wander round in due course, pre-warned and thus pre-armed with a small token birthday gift.

When we got there, we found that Paco and Fani were already there. Seeing us arrive, Loli announced her decision that we would, instead of sitting quietly on their terrace away from bright lights and civilisation, all make our way into Bullas, so that she could celebrate her birthday at La Cafetería Zalú.

We were as a result bundled into Pedro's car, to be unceremoniously bumped and rattled along the camino to Loli's chosen venue, which turned out to be an ice-cream parlour.

At half-past ten at night, therefore, we were sat round a couple of tables pushed together on the wide recreation area on the opposite side of the road from the cafeteria. Amongst dozens of other noisy groups of Spanish revellers scattered around at tables under the canopy of trees, beneath a large August moon, we toasted Loli with obscenely large copas de helado of different flavours.

All that was missing, really, was the jelly and the tantrums.

This soirée did make me feel much better about the break-in, however. To a man, all the other members of our party were firmly of the opinion that this was the random act of an opportunist thief, merely stealing copper to weigh in, rather than the deliberate continuation of a vendetta. I questioned the sanity of a thief who would risk so much for so little, but Fani told us about a friend of hers with the usual weekend place in the campo, fully equipped, who suffered a break-in and broken door latch merely to discover that the thief had been more than happy to take and eat just three bananas.

Apparently, he even left the skins.

John and Pedro are turning into soul mates. While we were indulging in our ice-creams, Pedro pointed out the group of little old men sat on the benches in the shadows at the periphery of the trees, leaning on their sticks, deep in conversation as they enjoyed the cooler, fresher evening air.

"That'll be us," he said to John, "When we are old."

Yes, I can just see them in the corner of a bar somewhere, moaning to each other about the youth of today and playing dominoes, or on the terrace of the centro de pensionistas, dribbling and gurning.

The Guardia Civil & Upsetting the Pedros

When I visited the rather imposing offices of the Guardia Civil in Bullas to report the breaking and entering of our property and the subsequent theft of some two metres of electric cable, I was surprised that the officer who logged the denuncia announced that they would come to site the following day to have a look.

So we duly hung around all day Sunday for these guys to arrive, but it will probably come as no great surprise to learn that they didn't. Neither did we hear from them on Monday – or at least, not until gone half-past eleven at night, when I received a mobile phone call asking precisely where we were.

I gave directions, somewhat taken aback - primarily that they were intending to visit at such an unearthly hour, and secondly that they don't know their own small town inside out. Meanwhile John was pointing with some mirth at the distant blue light making its way back towards town from El Salto, clearly returning from a trip along the wrong track altogether.

So, on a very dark night at some time approaching midnight, with the outside of the house washed by their car headlights, the police checked out an insignificant burglary inside the house, inspecting with interest the severed and mutilated cable by the illumination from a feeble solar torch - a surreal scene that somehow served to make the whole incident somehow Hitchcockian.

The inspection of the damage took, as could easily have been predicted, less than two minutes – however, they chose to stay for the best part of an hour, discussing with us the beautiful spot in which we would be living, and the course of events leading to the sealing of the house, and the fact that we shouldn't be worried (classic Spanish). In retrospect, I suppose they were probably waiting for the offer of a coffee, or a beer, but it's a decent hike uphill back to the caravan so I'm afraid they got neither.

As it happens, I caught them in the petrol station today buying lollipops, so perhaps coffee or beer would have been too sophisticated anyway.

Pedro is currently handing to me, over the fence, tomatoes the size of my head at the rate of half a dozen a day. Now I like tomatoes, but there has got to be a physical limit to the number I am able to consume, especially when I am on my own half the time. I asked him what Loli does with them all, wondering if she perhaps turned them into gazpacho, or purée, or chutney – but no, Pedro informs me, they eat just one a day for almuerzo, and Loli preserves a few, but mainly they give them away. He prefers growing them to eating them, he confides.

As he passed me a bulging carrier bag-full recently, he and Pedro Junior were both stood at the fence commenting on (for which read criticising) some of our handiwork in a newly-formed "garden" area on the barn approach. They cannot understand why the British feel the need to straighten things up and prettify them in the way that we do – they regard it as totally unproductive, unnecessary and basically demented. Of course, Loli sees it differently, and it is probably the realisation that he is going to be in for some earache from her that makes Papa Pedro quite so scathing.

Anyway, while we were talking, Marcos was grubbing about in the soil at my feet digging out and eating large ants. This caught Pedro's eye and seemed to amuse him no end, so the subject was changed, to my relief, and Marcos became the focus of attention. I was asked how old he is now, and the conversation ran on for a few minutes about how a five-month-old puppy could possibly be standing at mid-thigh height already. Pedro then commented that there seems to be some animosity between Marcos and Qivi, and warned that there might arise in the future some bloody battles for supremacy.

"Don't worry," I said, innocently. "Just as soon as Alfonso the vet deems the time to be right, I will have him castrated."

Good grief! You'd have thought by their joint reaction that I had just stated my intention to cut out my grandmother's heart and serve it lightly steamed on a bed of garlic mash at the next Saint's Day.

Their first reaction, of course, what with them being Spanish, was to clutch their own testicles, as if this action would somehow put a barrier charm around Marcos' own little bulbs and protect him from the pain and the indignity I was aiming to visit gleefully upon him.

Then they both writhed around a little in a kind of badly synchronised dance routine, as though the very thought of such agony was giving them a group bout of serious gonadal discomfort.

Then they both shouted at me for a full five minutes.

Apparently it is not God's will that we should neuter animals, and I am therefore heathen and barbaric. I was informed at length and at volume that I would stunt his growth (oh, ha ha) and shorten his (miserable) life, and he would hate me forever.

I returned to the caravan feeling like an exceedingly sinful child caught pulling the wings off insects.

I feel the need to make a point here, though. I fail utterly to understand the Spanish mentality on this issue. The number of homeless dogs straying around in packs all over Spain bears witness to the fact that many Spanish think just as the Pedros do about castration. But I cannot for the life of me reconcile this attitude on the one hand with the one on the other that allows poncily-dressed pseudo-dancers to stick dozens of spears into a drugged bull. Nor the one that permits cages packed full of live rabbits to be left outside stores to bake in full sun before some wicked old witch selects one to carry home by its back legs, wriggling and struggling, to have its brains bashed out (humanely? somehow, I doubt it) ready for the preparation of arroz con conejo.

The misplaced sensitivity demonstrated in the first case seems so diametrically opposed to the utter sadism of the other two situations that I just don't get it.

I phoned Alfonso, so thoroughly disturbed was I by the sheer force of their reaction, to check the points about stopping Marcos' meteoric growth rate, and the likelihood of bringing about an earlier death through castration.

"Rubbish," quoth Alfonso, "Castrated males grow more, if anything, and castration is obviously going to prevent the testicular cancer that's common in old and entire dogs."

So I will be continuing with my previous cutting-room plans regardless of the weight of public opinion from the guys next door. In the meantime, the Pedros now look at me a little more warily, in case I am harbouring other insane ideas for population control amongst homo sapiens. And for some inexplicable reason they both seem to stand corkscrewed sideways from the waist down these days when talking to me - in case I suddenly lunge at them to grab their balls and wrench off the protective charms, perhaps.

I will, of course, not be mentioning the "C" word again in their presence. I am, however, dreading the fury that will be unleashed upon me when comes the time for Marcos to be vacuuming up his ants from the inside of an Elizabeth collar.

Litter & Harvests

My friend Donna has had three visitors to stay with her lately, and we met up a couple of times while they were here for a bite to eat. During the course of general conversation, they managed to make me realise just how "Spanish" I have become in the last four years when they took me completely by surprise with disdainful comments on the propensity of the Spanish to throw litter around.

During their stay, they had visited a couple of sites of historical interest and were deeply dismayed by the amount of picnic residue that lurked there unattended, attracting flies and rats and despoiling rather good photo opportunities.

They went on to say how they were all especially unimpressed with the state of the floor in any Spanish bar during the course of almuerzo

I suppose, if I pause to think back, I have to admit that this grated immensely on my nerves too in the early days. Wading through used and discarded serviettes, dogends, newspapers, empty fag packets, crisp bags and so forth to reach the bar was at one time very off-putting, and did not appear to reflect at all well on the general hygiene of the place. John would, once upon a time, habitually march into a bar, take one look at the floor, and then turn on his heel and march back out, refusing even to drink amongst the mess, let alone eat. However, if you look at it logically, I suppose the location of those items on the floor means that they are not on the bar or tables, and are therefore in fact as far removed from the food and drink as they can be. Furthermore, anyone who hangs around to see the end of almuerzo will also witness the scrupulous daily sweeping and mopping of the floor thereafter.

I'm not excusing the modus operandi here – I'm merely saying that I am now so used to it that I don't turn a hair at the fact that the Spanish truly believe that the floor is just a huge waste paper basket, any more than I do that they do not think twice about smoking while preparing food, or about dogs, cats and sparrows lurking optimistically around tables while people are eating.

I wonder what the three ladies in question would have made of a bar we visited with John's dad Mike before he died, and his wife Anne, in the old quarter of Mula, then? Mike had specifically requested that we avoid any establishment that smacked of anglicisation and make instead for a "truly Spanish" bar. We found somewhere that fitted the bill to the letter on a steep old cobbled street in Mula, so we picked our way through the floor art to a (relatively) clear table, and ordered tapas and wine.

The décor was shabby, the interior dim, and it was noisy with speech and with the roll of slot machines, but the food was excellent. As we were eating, we each became aware that something was brushing round our legs and rifling through the litter below the table. We ignored it, expecting it to be the usual dog or cat that would move on quickly after gleaning whatever was available, but it became apparent that this was a more persistent scavenger and was actually waiting for us to offer to share with it our repast.

So I peered into the gloom below the table to locate the thing and eject it forcibly, and found myself confronted by... the bar ferret. Yes, it could only be Spain.

It is the time of the almond harvest. As I've said, our trees have seen better days and need, in the main, to be removed completely, to be replaced with new stock. But we have harvested our modest crop this year nonetheless, and have in consequence spent several days manually removing the green outer husks – and then several nights prising all the sticky goo from beneath our fingernails.

Most of the folk round here own, even if it is amongst a small co-operative group, a dehusking machine, into which the whole green furry fruit goes, and out of which comes the clean nut in its hard shell. Friends of ours, Rosanna and Richard, have purchased such a machine this year, after a mammoth manual de-husking last year of some two thousand kilos finished weight of almonds. Pedro also has one, and both were kindly placed at our disposal – but we felt that our paltry amount of almonds would scarcely warrant the starting of the tractor that drives the mechanism, so we set to with our bare hands.

All the town folk seem to have almond trees tucked away somewhere, too. The town currently looks something like a karting track – large rectangles of almonds are laid out in a sort of patchwork motif to dry in the sun in the street at the front of various houses, reaching halfway across the road and posing a real hazard for the unwary motorist.

We are also knee-deep in figs at the moment, along with every man and his wife and dog in Spain, I think. If we offer a bagful of figs to anyone they immediately pull that face of imminent stomach-emptying, and then they offer us a bagful of figs in return. There is, let's face it, a limited amount of scope for the use of the fresh fig. Especially as they are one of those incredibly awkward and disobliging fruits that will sit rock-hard and unyielding on the branch one minute and then hurl themselves melodramatically floorwards to an incredibly squidgy end the next.

Marcos thinks he's got it sorted, though. He has decided, somewhere in his little doggy brain, that ripe fig shampoo is just the thing for large hairy dogs. He therefore spends his entire time either rolling joyfully in the sticky pink pulp or squirming around uncooperatively under the hose.

In fairness, he is very soft and sweet-smelling in consequence…

Keeping Up Appearances

I have already had cause to mention the Spanish propensity for child-like staring; I also feel the need to remark on the similarly ingenuous Spanish habit of passing judgemental personal comments based on their own extremely set ways, since this very habit reared its head recently.

Friend and fellow parrot-owner Lisa, whom I met by chance via random e-mails about parrots over a year ago and who, by one of those remarkable coincidences in this small world also lives in Bullas, was telling me recently about the hurtful "telling-off" she once received from her neighbours here. Apparently she was taken to one side and admonished for her abysmal self-neglect when picking up the kids from school because she failed to dress up and to apply make-up in order to carry out this high-profile task. It would appear that such carelessness is a heinous crime here in Spain, since the Spanish mothers all doll up to the nines before gathering to scoop up the fruits of their loins, and she was obviously letting the side down badly.

Of course, it doesn't seem to matter a jot that an hour or so after the school-gate spew each day every one of them will be back at home in their housecoats and slippers tearing their hair out surrounded by screaming kids and looking for all the world like the dog's dinner … after regurgitation.

She was further reprimanded for wearing sandals (in her own house) in October. It just isn't done, she was told – sandals are for summer, and she should now be in shoes like all the Spanish women. When she objected that the ambient temperatures were still in the mid-twenties, and anyway, she was indoors and out of sight, she was answered with a shrug and advice to the effect that people were laughing at her.

Now Lisa is made of stern stuff, but she admits that, at the time, this upset her. It is hard enough settling into a new country and culture, what with the necessity of having to learn the language pretty damn quickly, and to assimilate all the requisite information to become registered and functional within the community, without having to live in fear that careless attention to appearance may cause lasting offence, or worse, may leave a wake of people wetting themselves at your expense.

I am amazed. This, from a nation of people who still think that the mullet is a trendy hairstyle…

A step further along this path leads to the issue of demarcation of the sexes here.

Another friend of mine, Shari, gave birth to her first child just over a year ago here in a Spanish hospital. She tells me that she was looked after excellently, and that the experience was really pleasurable, despite an awful lot of the scare-mongering stories that are bandied about, generally in the local English press.

However, she tells me that she did have cause to become extremely upset post-partum when she overheard, in her pleasantly drugged state, the two midwives talking to each other whilst bearing away her beautiful new baby daughter Mia. As they disappeared through the delivery room doors, the word that lingered behind them and managed to penetrate Shari's haze was "pendientes" (earrings).

It is a ritual carved in stone here in Spain that baby girls have their ears pierced immediately to identify them as girls. But Shari, being of the firm opinion that Mia should be allowed, in due course, to make her own decisions about perforations in her body, was adamant that at that stage her ears should remain entirely intact. Dissolving into floods of tears, then, she sent hubby Martin scurrying off through the corridors of the hospital to intercept them and to carry out a piercing-prevention manoeuvre.

Since then, Shari tells me, Mia could be dressed like candy-floss from head to toe in pink frills and bows, but the Spanish will still refer to her as "him" since the earrings are missing.

Strangely enough, this exact topic came up again a few days ago in a conversation I had with Teresa, a Spanish friend. She noticed that I had two holes in each ear lobe (a hangover from University days, when it was cool to have extra piercings but before the days of nose, tongue, lip, eyebrow or nipple rings) but that I was wearing nothing in either.

"Why two holes?" she inquired.

I shrugged. "It was fashionable when I did it."

"But no earrings," she continued.

Deborah Fletcher

"I can rarely be bothered," I replied. "Anyway, it's almost impossible with my mob – earrings make great but painful psittacine toys!"

"But you are such a strange person," she told me candidly. "Are you not worried that people will not realise that you are a woman?"

Well, let me think. Perhaps I'm relying a little too heavily on the size 38C boobs to be a bit of a give-away?

Some Results

I am finally able to declare that my spider bite has healed. Okay, it took six months. And it has left a hideously deformed scar on the outside of my left calf – it looks as though the Inquisitors did indeed set to with a branding torch to elicit the names of the faithless - although I can report that my leg was supremely brave and uttered not a word.

I'm actually quite fond, in a perverse way, of this scar, now that I've lived with the wound for so long. I have even threatened to have a tattoo of a spider done next to it as a memento. John has threatened divorce.

Rent-a-Stupid (Marcos) is also now six months old. The adjective "huge" really is woefully weak as a descriptor. He sucks up and devours anything in his manic path, like an omnivorous tornado. His motto is, "If it moves, eat it. If it doesn't move, make it move."

Since we felt that we really were obliged to save the world from further donkey-mammoth combos with his dementia, he has now been castrated, but you really wouldn't be able to tell – he hasn't faltered

I'm quite seriously thinking of buying a yoke and harness for him, as back-up to the dis-tractor.

Cookie continues to create havoc, in his own inimitable little way, but then if he failed to do so, he would inevitably be drummed unceremoniously out of the cockatoo union, whose five-point parrot mantra is as follows:

1. If I saw it first, it's mine to destroy.

2. If it's in my mouth, it's mine to destroy.

3. If I have to climb to get it, it's mine to destroy.

4. If you are playing with something and you put it down, it automatically becomes mine to destroy.

5. If it's broken, it's all yours.

So everything runs normally on that front.

And our time has come. D-day is finally upon us – this being "Decision Day", or maybe "Despair Day", or even "Do I Care Any More? Day".

The venerable gentlemen of the ayuntamiento, after a mere fifteen months of careful deliberation about our illegally-reformed casa, have finally arrived at a decision regarding the sanction.

I am very pleased to report that they have, in their infinite wisdom, decided that it would be inappropriate to demolish the house. I am relieved to hear this, since a decision to the contrary would have involved mass news coverage of an ugly scene depicting me handcuffed to the walls of the house as the bulldozers advanced, possibly holding aloft a sacrificial platter bearing the four testicles belonging jointly to el Concejal and el cabrón.

I would have accepted a demolition decision (relatively) gracefully had it been made when the whole issue came to light and the house was still at box stage, but I would not have taken it lying down after we had been encouraged by the Mayor His Very Self to spend another large sum of money to roof and clad the place, and to install windows.

Anyhow, it is to remain standing. It will still be illegal – that is, we are unable to incorporate it into our deeds – for another four years. (Although we will still have to pay local rates on the place... how does that work?)

But, since we have no intention of selling it, its current status poses us no problem whatsoever.

We have been charged a five-figure fine for contravention of local planning laws, but we are informed that there is a reduction of 50% if we pay it immediately, which brings it down to a mere four-figure fine.

Although our house was, as far as we were concerned, inadvertently built without the correct permissions, this whole process and result make it clear to me why all the Spanish continue to build illegally by choice. Given that the planning application fees would have cost us something very close to the value of the fine, and that we are now assured that the application process can take several years, it's really no surprise that they just get on with it and face the consequences later. Still, it's not a situation in which I would like to find myself again.

Although never forget that we do still have the barns to tackle...

During this week, little white tents have sprung up like mushrooms all over Bullas, along with a huge structure that has swallowed whole the car park. There is also an abundance of fairy lights and flags strung across the streets, all in preparation for the momentous celebrations this coming weekend of the Bullas Fiesta del Vino.

As far as I'm concerned, the timing couldn't have been more apposite, and I will be taking part with gusto when Donna and I go to watch Jose in drag (and if you're trying to imagine that, picture Dame Edna Everidge crossed improbably with Gollum) singing his little heart out in the grand marquee at eleven o'clock on Saturday night, whilst sampling a few of the local fermentations and toasting the future.

The Birds, The Birds

I recently made my way home from the airport during a late October evening into an absolutely vivid and glorious autumn dusk. To the west, marching along a classic Mediterranean skyline, were the black silhouettes of tall palm trees reaching exactly as they should into a pink and orange firmament framed by deep turquoise darkening to indigo. Completing the picture, as is only right and proper, were the myriad dark specks of birds streaming southwards before the cold winter weather envelops this land in earnest.

There was, however, a jarring note in this idyllic scene. While the colourful skies were behaving themselves perfectly, with all the hues merging beautifully in all the right places, and the black palms were waving obligingly and elegantly in perfect time, driven by the fresh breeze, I was dismayed to note that the flocks of migrating birds were flying in V-shaped formations as sharp and as clean as warm blancmanges. Never before have I witnessed such a straggly, unkempt and frankly disgraceful display. I can only imagine that, charged with the mission of fetching along the Christmas duty-free to their southern relatives, these aviators, to a bird, had sampled one too many in the Spanish bodegas.

I have just had reason to spend a substantial amount of time watching birds flying overhead in the area local to the caravan, too. A loud and unexpected firework, let off early one morning for no apparent reason whatsoever, put the fear of God into the parrots and caused Jack, the African grey, and the little cockatiel Joey, to take flight through the open barn door. Both were clipped, and neither were in good flying form since they never really had the opportunity to practise, but the strong thermals in the valley were obviously enough to give them lift and we watched horrified as both soared up and disappeared from view.

The area here is densely covered with tall pine trees, and the terrain is mountainous, folded, and ideal for two birds to lose themselves thoroughly. It was therefore with a heavy heart and next-to-no hope of recovery that I turned out to hunt for them.

We had a rough idea of their outward-bound direction, and I know that domestic parrots will usually stay within a mile radius of home for at least a week, but still the task seemed more daunting than the proverbial needle in a whole county full of haystacks.

John was obliged to fly back to the UK that same day, so when I turned out the following morning I was accompanied by Lisa and Donna, who, troopers that they are, arrived early on my doorstep and spent all morning trudging round the near neighbourhood letting the bemused farmers know of my losses, and handing out phone numbers on the off-chance that any one of them should spot either of the birds. To no avail, of course.

The following day, Donna and I went out even earlier, before dawn, with the idea that we would drive a little way into the suspect area and holler at the tops of our lungs as the sun came up, as recommended by internet sites on lost parrots . On our way, we spotted a patrolling Policía Local car, so I screeched to a halt in front of it, leapt from my car and waved them down. Poor guys; they blanched visibly at the vision of an ungroomed and clearly demented Englishwoman coming at them from the dark flailing like a windmill, but they gamely took details and said they'd pass them on to the forest rangers further up into the mountains. They also gave me permission to put up some "Lost" posters (which is handy, because I was going to do that anyway).

But it turned out to be another fruitless journey.

On the way home, disheartened and thirsty, we made our last port of call with the posters to a local dog kennels, probably less than three hundred metres downstream from me as the crow (or parrot) flies but much further by road. I knew that this was run by an English lady I had never previously met. Mavis, who has subsequently become a good friend, had her daughter Trina and four grandchildren Tom, Becky, Lewis and Chelsea staying with her, and all agreed to keep a keen eye out for my wayward birds.

That same day, Lisa and I had arranged to travel down to La Casa de Coko, a parrot sanctuary in Cartagena, about an hour away, to pick up a new bird I was adopting. This adoption had arisen following a prior visit to the sanctuary in which Lisa had conducted an interview for a magazine article she was writing for her North West Murcia Gazette, and I acted as her photographer. Noodle, a green Indian Ringneck parrot, provided one of the star photos. She is a disturbed little bird who has plucked herself right down to oven-ready chicken with a big green pom-pom head (which part she physically can't reach to pluck, or she would) and I fell in love with her, even though she would surely take out my jugular if I was incautious with her.

So we drove down to pick her up, with me feeling immensely fraudulent to be taking a new feathered friend into my care when I was clearly an unfit mother hen.

Lisa stopped for a coffee when we arrived back at the caravan, and then disappeared with the promise of extra help the following day in the great hunt.

As her taillight disappeared around the bend of the camino, the phone rang. It was Mavis.

"I think we can see your African grey in a tree just across the river. He's been whistling and calling, and the kids have been calling back to him to keep him interested".

I got there within three minutes (the Policía Local were fortunately somewhere else) – and there, indeed, was Jack, perched at the very top of the highest pine I have ever seen.

Quivering with relief, I walked very slowly down towards the river until I was about ten metres away from the pine, looking up at Jack. I spoke to him, using the phrases and whistles we use to each other as "flock calls"; he looked down at me, with his head on one side, and whistled back. We kept up this interchange for about ten minutes, while I held aloft a peanut as an offering to tempt him down to me.

Then a car full of young Spaniards drove past at speed, with all the windows wide open, stereo blaring, making as much noise as only Spaniards can, and Jack took off.

I immediately took chase, along with Lewis and Chelsea, in the direction of his flight. This, for us, involved a frenzied scramble uphill from the river through all manner of undergrowth and brambles, insect nests and dog turds (I hope), in a vain attempt each to follow on two (clumsy) legs a creature soaring free on two wings. But we did manage to spot from afar his next landing place – a tree high up on the edge of a cliff at the bend in the river, beyond a fenced villa. Scrambling noisily across treacherous terrain towards the landward side of the villa, I saw a man with his back to me working in the gardens, and so I ran towards the fence to accost him and to ask him to watch the "gris con cola roja" (grey with red tail) in the tree on the other side of his place.

But as I hurtled towards him, and yelled, "¡Perdoneme, Señor!" I fell into a ditch immediately before his fence and disappeared entirely from view. The poor man spun, startled, to see absolutely nothing at all. The only evidence that he had been so rudely interrupted was the sound of gentle moaning from a point just below ground level beyond the fence.

I hoisted myself from the cleverly-concealed man trap and arose, now clad in an assortment of grasses and copious amounts of dust, with ripped trousers and beset by a severe limp where I had also torn something vital in my knee during the descent. I made my request about vigilance with regard to the bird in the tree… that was no longer there. Bugger.

We limped back forlornly to Mavis, who announced that Jack had flown back full circle and was somewhere nearby. So we agreed that I would bring his cage to the kennels courtyard and leave it there with food and water in the hope that he was running short of both.

For four more days we continued our look-out. The kids were marvellous – they'd heard my whistles and the expressions I used with Jack, and they used them repeatedly to keep him focussed on the courtyard and his cage. Each morning, I would arrive just before dawn, with Cookie Cockatoo– who was not best pleased about the early mornings and was getting increasingly bad-tempered about the whole thing, but who would, therefore, let forth a tirade of abuse as we arrived which aroused Jack's interest immensely. We would talk to Jack for up to an hour each day, before he took off into the wild blue yonder just to underline the point that he was free so to do.

On the morning of day five, Jack sat at the top of the Washingtonia palm tree in the courtyard and talked to us for ages before soaring off. And looking, I have to say, so beautiful and natural in flight that I felt (still feel) pangs at the thought of him caged.

But the day turned nasty, as low cloud came in and thunder rumbled ominously in the distance. That evening, the thunder and lightning were much closer, and the rain heavy, so that when I made my way to the kennels, there was no sign of him at all, and I returned to the caravan after a couple of hours' vigil without any sightings and completely dispirited. I spoke to John that evening, and told him that I though we'd lost him for good, in that the weather had probably forced him to take cover in the denser forest higher up. I was also ever-fearful of the large birds of prey overhead.

I said that I would give it one more day.

The following morning, I got there early as usual; the kids were already all up and about in their pyjamas, and were telling me that they were returning to the UK that evening but that they really didn't want to go until we got Jack back. I told them that I was in agreement and not to worry, because I would be keeping them hostage until his return, as they were doing such a fine job of communication with him.

Mavis made me a coffee, and I stood outside in the drizzle, while the kids hovered about under the porch, buzzing.

We spent about twenty minutes making all the usual noises and calls to Jack, with no response. I was now convinced that I had been correct the previous evening - he'd gone. I drank my coffee morosely, wandered over to his empty cage and took out a handful of sad-looking wet peanuts without enthusiasm.

"Jack wanna peanut?" I called out over the persistent patter of the rain, holding aloft a soggy and unappetising sample. "Wanna peanut?"

"Oh", replied Jack, from a low palm branch about two metres up and some five metres away from me.

I froze. The kids froze. The rain continued.

"Hello, Jack. Love you."

"Love you", replied Jack.

"Wanna peanut?" I repeated, turning slowly and holding one out directly to him, as I started to inch carefully, cautiously closer, talking softly to him all the while. The kids, bless them, remained utterly still and as silent as church mice. After what felt like an eternity, I stood below him, almost near enough to touch him. He dipped his head and I gently reached the peanut up to him, just far enough away from his beak to make him strain down a little way for it, which, after only brief hesitation, he did.

And I grabbed him. He bit me, but not too hard, as if to say, "Okay, I'm ready to come home, get dry, eat and sleep in safety – but don't take it for granted".

The kids screamed loud and long, and danced around in their PJs in the rain like some demented heathen tribe giving thanks, with Trina watching aghast, knowing that she had to dry all their clothes before leaving. I, to my everlasting mortification, howled like a baby. It was a fantastic end to the kids' holiday, and Trina took them home happy.

I never saw Joey again, though.

They Just Don't Care

Driving home from the market in town this morning with my rubbish riding passenger in the back of the car, I turned into the camino and almost ran straight into a man stood very still with his back to me at the edge of the road, facing the field and adopting that clearly defined hands-clasped-prayerlike-together-below-waist-level, legs-ever-so-slightly-parted stance that just yells out, "¡Hombre pípí!"

This is something that, early on, requires some mental realignment here – the fact that the entire male population is of the belief that it is perfectly acceptable to unzip their fly and relieve themselves in full public view without feeling shame or (they think) giving offence.

They certainly don't do it to disgust. As far as I am aware, they don't do it in company, either – only when they are alone or can remove themselves to a decent distance from their workmates or friends. Nonetheless, they do not seem to feel the need to find a bush to conceal them in the act, as the more modest Englishman would probably do; neither do they deem it at all necessary to hold on until they reach the next bar. Like male dogs, they seem to see it as an inalienable right to leave their scent wherever the mood takes them.

As for me, I find that I just have this overwhelming desire to have an extra horn fitted to the car for such occasions that sounds like a donkey braying...

That general lack of modesty regarding all things private (by our standards) seems to pervade rural life here.

As I drive down the road that descends from the Bullas mound to the western exit of the carratera C415 when I'm going over to neighbouring Cehegín, there is a little row of tiny terraced houses on the left-hand side of the road that faces a large fenced piece of land on the right. The occupants of these houses, all elderly and fairly corpulent, clearly have no back yards, no balconies, and precious little space inside their casas pequeñas for the essential drying of washing. They have therefore claimed squatters' rights along a stretch of pavement on the opposite side of the road, and have rigged up a chain of washing lines against the fence bordering the land.

Upon these they peg a varied assortment of scary wet underwear – brassieres that could comfortably accommodate six-month old twins, knickers and underpants that would make passable bivouacs for enterprising boy scouts, string vests that look like assault course fixtures – and if the wind is from the north, blowing towards the houses, this motley collection flaps madly across half the road in a vain attempt to return home, straining against the pegs and slapping against the nearside windows of any cars daring or foolhardy enough to run the gauntlet. Not an attractive prospect.

Speaking of the absence of shame, I can also report that the Spanish make no apology for their driving skills (or lack thereof). I recently found myself caught unexpectedly in a mini-traffic jam on my way out of Bullas on the minor road that passes through the mountains to Totana. I imagined that I would find the cause to be a large herd of goats being shepherded by a goatherd and his two dogs across the road from one grazing zone to another, as is quite normal in these parts, but found instead as I slowly advanced that the delay was simply down to a Mercedes C520 nose-down in a ditch on the other side of the road. The driver, on the verge behind the misaligned car, was sat on a deckchair merrily eating sandwiches, with a large umbrella shading him from the sun, and he was holding court one at a time with each car that crawled past, acknowledging each enquiring driver by raising a can (soft drink, I assume, but I wouldn't bet my life on it) and exchanging a few words on the current state of affairs.

I felt that it would be surly merely to drive on past and ignore him, so I dutifully wound down my window as I drew level and said, "¡Hombre! ¡Mala suerte!" – at which he just grinned, saluting me with the can.

On the return journey, I was amused to note that Mercedes man was still in situ, but that he had been joined by the police – he, still sat on his deckchair, they leaning on the car roof, all with cans and clearly sharing a great joke, probably about the inability of roads in these parts to stay where they were put.

Not that the police have any room to talk. Waiting in a queue of traffic at the lights at the top of the Gran Vía in Cehegín last week, I just happened to glance to my left at the cars parked on the opposite side of the road one busy market morning, only to witness a police car leaving its space by reversing into the front of the car behind it, and then nonchalantly driving off. The offending driver must have caught my look of disbelief, as he winked at me and gave that head-half-cocked shrug of theirs.

One rule for one, eh?

I must point out, though, that despite the atrocious driving in Spain that we encounter far too often, I think that the Spanish are generally very good-natured drivers. I exclude, of course, the rampant young speed maniacs that have some great point or another to prove, because they will always (and anywhere in the world) sit hard on your tail and hassle you until they can screw past at some inappropriate time and at uncontrollable speed. But with them put aside, I have to say that I find drivers here to be a fairly laid-back and patient bunch. I am always pleased to find that cars are allowed, for instance, to slot in without great drama as they join major roads from the ridiculously short and poorly-signed slip roads. I compare this with the total lack of courtesy and the considerable amount of aggression I have encountered on the few occasions I have revisited the UK, where any attempt to join one road from another is met with intimidating gestures and much jostling as each driver does his utmost to make sure that he leaves not an inch of space that may allow someone to shoehorn themselves into the queue and join ahead of him.

I suppose that this is merely one aspect of the time pressures that people in the UK suffer (and I remember suffering also, but only as a long-distant echo of a memory suppressed heavily by ego-defence mechanisms that would kick and scream at the thought of having to return…)

So then I find myself wondering what, for instance, an office manager in the UK would have to say if he sent out the office junior to run an errand to the bank, and if that same junior was gone for nearly two hours? Probably a first verbal warning offence there, whereas here it would be nothing more than expected – we've all stood in line for the best part of a morning, waiting patiently for the one cashier in a bank to deal with a long "cola" (tail) of people, each with a whole stack of transactions and queries.

And in fact, the same office junior here would be considered fully justified in stopping for a coffee on the way back to the office, having had to wait for so long.

Life before work – such a fabulous and laudable philosophy!

The Season To Be Jolly

How civilised. I am just starting to see the trappings of Christmas appear: trees covered in baubles and tinsel, piles of wrapped and beribboned empty boxes in shop windows, Santa Clauses climbing/falling blind-drunk from a thousand balconies simultaneously, and of course the extensive (and environmentally-unfriendly) street light displays in every town.

And – good grief – it's already the beginning of December.

What a relief.

I was sick to the back teeth in the UK of the incessant high-pressure advertising of children's toys and Christmas fare, the blaring of Christmas carols from radio stations and shop doorways, the gaudy decorations and ridiculous festive costumes of shop staff, and all in November just as soon as the fireworks die. Or even earlier, in fact.

Somehow, I can again feel that it is actually a time of excitement and anticipation – a short spell of just a couple of weeks of overspending, overeating and forced bonhomie, kept alive by its brevity.

The religious aspect is also, of course, much more in evidence here, despite the large Muslim community from North Africa, which makes something of a mockery of the climate of deep fear in multi-cultural Britain and the "politically-correct" insanity that seems to accompany it.

Each year, a great many towns, in one of their main plazas, put on in the weeks before Christmas a still-life nativity scene with miniature figurines set in tiny villages on beautifully-constructed landscapes that cover a huge area – finely-detailed, fully-lit, even with moving parts and running water. Each town vies with its neighbours to create the most impressive display. These are all works of art – intricate, beautiful and emotive – and it is possible, I believe, to book a coach trip that takes in a number of them (and a couple of bars) during an evening tour of a given area, something I would like to do one Christmas when I am not firmly attached to one end of a brick-layer's trowel, or some such.

Of course, I am overlooking a couple of small but pertinent points in my summary of the protracted Christmas run-up in Britain, and I am probably being overly-harsh on them when at least it is true that they only do it once a year.

The Spanish, however, for whom the fiesta is paramount, manage to have two major Christmas celebrations. The first, being on Christmas eve, involves the giving and receiving of a token present some time after the evening indulgence at Christmas dinner with the entire four generations of local family, and before the obligatory attendance at midnight mass. This seems to be a respectful sort of affair, a marking of a significant time in a dignified fashion.

The second celebrates the delayed arrival of the Three Kings with their homage on January 6th. This one corresponds much more closely to the Christmas Day farcical nonsense of the ridiculous piles of overpriced and unnecessary presents that we have come to know and detest (am I, by the way, alone in recalling the excitement and pride in receiving a watch, for example, for Christmas, supported by a pillowcase-full of colouring books, paints, small board games, fruit and nuts?)

Spanish kids, if anything, seem to get even more big stuff – electronic, motorised, designer - than their British counterparts. And this particular celebration also gives rise to yet more time out of school for kids that frankly hardly ever seem to me to be in it.

And, of course, being Spain, it involves churches, costumes and loud bangs. Firstly, an elaborate live nativity tableau is set up inside the church, to depict the holy birth two weeks on. This is then invaded by three further cast members, toiling under heavy ornate tepees and sporting obscene amounts of facial hair, carrying three tiny boxes. They generally arrive on the back of some disreputable pick-up belching black smoke and back-firing loudly, and playing hideously-distorted tinny carols through an original Edison recording drum (or so it would seem). This close approximation to ancient Judean transport then loiters outside the church, still running, to await the disgorgement of the whole cast so that they can mount once more to be driven jerkily and unsteadily around the town. They are followed on foot by the entire Church congregation (that is, almost every member of the townfolk), and by the obligatory town nutter who carries under his very nose a small neck-slung tray full of the ground-to-air missiles that they call fire crackers here, which he lights in a launcher cradle perched on the front of the same tray. Clearly a man who can't get life insurance.

The very first time I ever witnessed this was when I was back in Sucina, and I was the only English person there (having been the very first to move onto the urbanisation by about three months). I took the two dogs with me for a walk and a nosey, and found myself loitering outside the church with the moody and sullen teenagers who were "not going in there, no way". I had fully intended to follow the ensuing procession respectfully with the dogs, to absorb the local colour. The dogs, however, had very different ideas; and with the first explosion from the nutter's tray, they both took off back towards home like startled wild horses, with me flying like a pennant in the wind behind them hanging on to the two leads for dear life, hoping they would land me gently.

One must not forget, either, that these two distinctly Christmassy affairs are neatly bisected by La Noche Vieja – New Year's Eve. I have spent this particular night a few years now with Spanish families, who have taken pity on me when John is inevitably on duty through the festive period, but I am still pretty useless when it comes to the time-honoured custom of trying to shovel down twelve whole (seed-filled) grapes in time with the twelve chimes of the clock as the witching hour arrives. Although I must admit that it beats by a long way the other regrettably popular custom of trying to shovel down as much alcohol as possible.

It still seems very strange to me, though, after celebrating the end of the old year and the subsequent launch of the new, to be looking at a second bout in the Christmas ring.

Full Circle

I recall - it was late September.

The myriad white tents that had appeared in order to sustain the throngs milling around at the bustling and highly-charged Bullas Fiestas, erupting overnight like teenage acne before a hot date, had flourished for their week of glory before disappearing back whence they came.

And I, in my eagerness to pay a huge fine for the illegal house building and then to get on with the finishing of same so that I could remove myself from my sardine tin and enjoy a semblance of normality again, had managed to overlook one huge universal truth about the Spanish.

They don't have any concept of "now".

Anyone who has ever had any dealings with the native countrymen here will be fully aware that they have two most favourite and very hackneyed sayings – "mañana, mañana", and "poco á poco".

These two phrases speak absolute volumes about the mentality here. Primarily, it would seem, that the Spanish are great fans of repetition; but also that tomorrow, tomorrow is always a better time to get anything done than today, today, and (very) little by (ridiculously) little is the best way to do it even then.

So when the 29th September deadline set for the issue of the resolution by the Ayuntamiento, as stipulated by themselves, came and went, I should not have been surprised in the slightest.

However, a year later, and still we are not in possession of the formal resolution document, nor the written demand for the fine. The Oficina Técnica told us (after much nagging) the extent of the damage back in September, and assured us that the resolution had been irrevocably decided, and further gave us El Concejal's permission therefore to finish our project, but to this day we have nothing in writing.

We have trusted him. This may seem foolish, in the light of our previous dealings, but we honestly have no choice whatsoever if we ever plan to occupy this house. We take solace from the fact that at least three neighbours in our vicinity are all in the same boat as us, and they have all busily resumed their labours having been given the same verbal green light as us. So we have followed suit.

Of course, that still doesn't mean that things get done quickly. Vicente, our electricista, is a devout follower of the "poco á poco", "mañana" or even "la semana que viene" creed, and therefore while he is a dear and obliging soul who has done a splendid job for us, he has still nevertheless taken almost six months to achieve what was expected (by us) to take a couple of weeks.

We have had to cajole and beg and threaten plasterers and tilers to come along and do their bit in timely fashion. The solar engineers are still not quite finished despite starting the job nine months ago. We have needed to place on order any number of fittings and furnishings that all seem, for some inexplicable reason, to take the magic number of twelve weeks to manufacture and deliver.

And even I, who thought I had everything covered and would very soon now achieve my modest goal of being able to climb in and out of a bed without kneecapping myself, had managed to overlook the minor fact that it would take me at least a month and close to a hundred litres of paint to coat all the fresh new plaster in every room. Spanish plaster has obviously descended directly from some dubious relationship between gypsum and a sea sponge, and if I never again see another paint roller in my life it'll be too soon.

Jenny, a professional therapist/masseuse and good friend from Cehegín, heroically offered to come over and help with this monumental task after I'd been to see her for some therapy to a neck utterly sick of looking at a ceiling at close quarters. She managed a couple of weekend sessions up a ladder and covered in splashes of cream paint before losing the will to live and hurling herself bodily from a moving rug, thus dislocating her patella and becoming unavailable for further input, leaving me to toil on alone.

I am therefore, a whole year on, still occupying the good old caravan. Meanwhile, the seasons have turned full circle, as is the nature of the thing, and once again I find myself in the middle of horrific and violent gale-force storms.

I had to rescue the dog kennels from my eastward neighbour's field this week. The strong westerly wind was gusting to such strengths that it had managed to pick them up and hurl them through the wooden ranch boundary fencing (smashing it to pieces in the process) before dumping them unceremoniously onto his land, which drops below ours and continues to slope downwards.

Fortunately, the dogs were not in residence at the time – although, on reflection, it might have been better had Marcos in fact been laying in his, since, being no Toto, he would in all likelihood have anchored it down firmly, even in a hurricane. Now a year old, he is weighing in at more than sixty kilos and still continues to munch anything even remotely edible in order to keep on track with his own self-imposed expansion programme.

And once again, I offer up thanks for John's wise insistence on anchor chains for the poor old caravan, which shudders and quakes its way through night after night of the punishing blows of the high winds and of the loose debris that they manage to pick up and carry with them specifically to hurl at me.

No real rain to speak of this year, though, at odds with the torrents of the stuff that I endured last year. We had none of the usual late January snow, either, which utterly thwarted the usual influx of visitors, who normally come from far and wide to enjoy the pleasures of making yeti prints in the thick crunchy layers of the rare white flakes, and to carry away proudly a trophy snowman mounted on the car bonnet.

So it is probably safe to say that we are in for a parched and uncomfortable summer.

Polla Asada & Other Health Issues

L earning a second language is full of pitfalls, especially for the British who are, let's face it, notoriously bad at it.

Spanish throws up many an opportunity for confusion, with any number of words being very similar in both look and sound but not in meaning.

For example, cabello (hair) is close enough to caballo (horse), which in turn is painfully similar to caballa (mackerel), and a non-speaker could even be forgiven for confusing any one of them with cebolla (onion).

This is all harmless, of course, and while it may well elicit bemused looks, it would certainly not cause offence.

However, there are, naturally, other mistakes to be made that are a little nearer to the knuckle.

For example, when my dear friend Christine went to a furniture shop in search of a tallboy, she prepared herself before-hand to ask for "un armario con cajones" (a cupboard with drawers). It would have worked, possibly, had she remembered correctly the phrase she had set out to say – but instead, she asked for "un armario con cojones", which, to her utter consernation, left the shop staff in helpless hysterics on the floor. She had, unbeknown to her until later, asked for a cupboard with testicles.

Along the same lines, I must report the instance of another friend, who shall remain nameless although she knows who she is, with whom I took lunch fairly recently. She decided that, of the menú del día options available, she would quite like for her main course the "pollo asado" (roast chicken). However, when came the time to place her order, she spoke without consulting the menú, and thus managed to distort it to "polla asada".

I smirked at the waiter, who, bless him, smirked back but managed otherwise to keep a straight face. And he did serve her roast chicken – largely, I feel, because that not even for the comedic value were the kitchen staff prepared to volunteer the appropriate part to serve her what she had ordered, which was in fact that Chinese speciality "crispy roast dick". (And that's not a typo).

I haven't until now pointed this out to her – mainly because I've been waiting with interest to see if she will make the same mistake again and if, further, there is an obliging chef out there somewhere…

We almost produced a donor yesterday.

John was nearly decapitated.

We had the day before ordered a wagon-load of gravel to be delivered to site, in order to fill the hole around the new depuradora installed to serve the house. The wagon driver, Miguel, who has been here with deliveries of materials far more times than he would care to count, is an obliging and cheerful little guy who has always been prepared to leave the camino and to drive his lorry precariously along various terraces in order to deposit the load as close to a point of requirement as he can.

So yesterday he drove along the terrace below the house and past the depuradora, so that he could then back up to the hole and dump the entire contents straight in.

John stood behind the wagon, by the hole, to signal to Miguel when to cease reversing. All well and good – with the lorry perfectly positioned, John opened the tailgate and Miguel began to raise the tipper.

The gravel shifted, and began to slide down. As the tipper bed reached an angle of about 45°, suddenly and without warning, the whole bed detached itself from the wagon and slid off at speed, narrowly missing John's head before crashing onto the top of the new depuradora.

Miguel shot out of his cab like a bullet, puce-coloured and shaking like a jelly in an earthquake. His knees were literally knocking and barely able to support him, and we feared for his heart. John, the almost-victim, was unscathed and just a little shocked, but Miguel was a complete mess.

"Let me get you some water," said John, but Miguel shook his head. "Whisky, then," offered John.

"No, no, no," Miguel squeaked. "Un cigarillo…"

Health and safety matters here in Spain are something that happen somewhere else. It is nothing to walk along a street here with a moving crane overhead swinging a hopper-full of wet cement, or to pass a builder's skip deposited alongside a building under renovation and suddenly have a piece of rubble whistle past your ear as it is dropped from an upper floor into the skip. If you twist your ankle in a pothole in the pavement, then how very stupid of you! Don't even think of going to the Ayuntamiento to complain (let alone sue!) You're a big person now - just watch your step more carefully in future.

More questionable still is the situation where the Spanish pay lip-service only to the obligation to apply various European health and safety directives (those that they choose not to ignore entirely, that is). For example, the need to provide access for the disabled can be seen to have been obeyed by many a bar here in the shape of a small ramp installed begrudgingly half-way across the entrance steps leading up to the bar. But the ramp, having to do the job of three short steps, therefore ends up at a gradient of something like 1 in 1. Assuming, of course, that they had the strength to heave themselves up it and into the (crowded) bar in the first place, this ramp can only serve to pitch some poor wheelchair-bound customer leaving the bar right into the middle of the road and under the wheels of a bus!

The public smoking issue is another risible one. When the Europe-wide ban of smoking in public places was drawn up, legislation was passed in Spain stipulating that any bar or restaurant with a floor area of over $100m^2$ is required to provide a separate enclosed area for smokers. Smaller places may opt to allow smoking or not, at the owner's discretion.

Personally, I am dismayed to find that a great many of these places seem to have been measured with an elastic tape measure, and therefore the legislation does not appear to have made an ounce of difference to the smoking habits of the native Spanish.

But at least it is generally accepted that there is so much less stress here.

Unless you are disabled or a non-smoker, that is...

Deborah Fletcher

More Beasties

Yes, I am probably certifiably insane. We can barely afford to buy all the treatments required monthly for the three dogs and the cat to keep at bay the incredibly aggressive ticks here, let alone the food to keep them all from death's door (especially Marcos' share). So why, then, did I take in a little stray kitten just after Christmas? A kitten that didn't look as though he would make it through the week, suffering with feline virus and a whole bouquet of secondary bacterial infections, as well as ulcers in the mouth, the nose, the ears, the eyes…

Because, as has already been pointed out, I am a sucker for lost causes.

Ash, as he is called in deference to his colouring and in a puerile attempt to match him up with Smokie, pulled through after a week of intense nursing (and a daily visit to see Alfonso, which ultimately cost me some 200€). A scraggy, weak, pathetic little creature who had known nothing but pain and misery in his short life to that point, we allowed him to reside on a cushion in the caravan with us, kept him warm, drugged and hand-fed him.

The result is a bouncy, fluffy, happy, cheeky little hell-cat who terrorises his big sister and Jade, who narrows his eyes if he is told "no", who likes nothing better than to jump off the wall onto a passing back, or stretch lovingly from a lap up to a chin and bite it, who jumps up onto a

158

work surface and deliberately knocks everything onto the floor. Who gets into any car or van that should visit here, who winds himself affectionately around any stranger who subsequently just will not believe us when we say that he is the devil incarnate.

The only residue of the feline virus is his permanent snottiness, which at least gives forewarning of his approach, but otherwise he is in the rudest of health.

His one nemesis is Marcos-shaped. Marcos, being exceedingly delusional and of the impression that he is just a little puppy himself, likes to play with Ash by ironing him flat, Tom and Jerry style.

I have also taken to feeding and treating a neighbour's dog. Manoli, who is Loli's sister and has a place next door to Loli and Pedro, lives, like her sister, elsewhere in Bullas, but again like her sister, keeps dogs here in the campo premises. Her dog is a husky-cross-German shepherd (-ish), a big and gentle bitch by the name of Irena. Irena is not speyed (since it is not God's will) and is therefore pregnant twice a year, each time by an unknown father.

The last sire appears to have been a Doberman, I would guess, from the look of the puppies, which were as huge as the baby Marcos. Manoli managed to find places for all but one, to whom we refer as "Boy".

Boy wanders around in the camino, ever hopeful that he will be allowed inside Manoli's place to be with his mum, and he gets fed sporadically by Manoli's (dreadful) son, who comes, in his noisy car with his even noisier stereo blasting out, to feed Irena daily.

I was initially worried that Boy didn't seem to have a ready supply of fresh water, so we started putting out a bowl each day for him. Then, as he got bigger but thinner, I started to leave him some food to supplement anything he might be getting from Stereo Kid.

Eventually, he decided that he likes us, since we are here most of the time and are frequently outside, talking to him, so he approached us and began to sit with us wherever we happened to be working. It was then, reaching out to stroke him one day and snatching my hand back hastily in disgust, that I realised that he was absolutely smothered in ticks of all sizes – little black baby ones, massively-engorged huge yellow ones, and all things in-between. They were even ranked across his muzzle in rows, like fish fins. So I used a phial of Frontline drops, Marcos size, to treat him.

I can't physically take him in – Marcos and Qivi are not especially tolerant of other dogs, and anyway, Manoli hasn't officially relinquished him. But we do feel a responsibility now. And at least he remains tick-free and fed.

The parrot quota is also up. Oven-ready Noodle arrived in October, as I have already mentioned. It took me a good three months, and hands that looked liked they had suffered an attack by a killer mincing machine, before I could handle her, but she lets me stroke her at any time now, although I still have to watch her body language very carefully (which is, I admit, easier when it is denuded of feathers).

She is happy and settled enough to have laid me a clutch of six eggs already, and she occasionally leaves alone her feather regrowth until it begins to look promising – but then she strips all the pin feathers out again in one overnight session and we're back to square one. I'm so used to her looking like a miniature dinosaur, though, that I think it would be strange to see her fully-clothed!

I have also taken on a second African grey, named J.T. His owners Peter and Marion had no choice but to return to the UK, for health reasons, and Peter sorrowfully handed his beloved parrot to me for safe-keeping.

J.T. had always been caged, and Peter warned me that he would bite.

Now I don't hold with (in fact, I seriously hate) parrots being kept in small cages, and even in large cages they need time out, plus regular handling. So when J.T. arrived here with us his cage was opened up pretty quickly for him to come out and explore.

It took me about thirty seconds to realise that he is blind.

After almost nine years of permanent incarceration, he knew the inside of his cage like the back of his wing, so his disability wasn't apparent to Peter and Marion. He could hear when someone approached and stuck their fingers through the bars, and he would lunge in that general direction (as I suppose any nervous creature, sighted or unsighted, would do) and bite, if he could make contact. But out of the cage, and disorientated, it was immediately transparently evident to me that he couldn't see.

And he has turned out to be an absolute little darling. I make sure I'm always talking to him as I approach him, telling him what I'm doing. I rub my fingers together as I put my hand near his head, and he reaches into them for a scratch. He gives kisses to order, and he steps up nicely when I put my flattened hand up against his chest. I have to approach perches slowly with him on my hand so that he just touches his beak against them in order to locate them and clamber up, and I rattle his seed bowl as I hang it up for him, so that he can pinpoint it quickly.

He loves to hear the other birds going about their daily manoeuvres, chattering and whistling, and has already started to add his tuppence-worth. And his favourite pastime is basking in the sun.

It broke my heart when I first realised he was blind, and it still bothers me to see his area so devoid of the toys that fill all the others, but now I'm extremely glad that he has come to me, and that he appears to be happy, and I can only hope that I have enhanced his life a little, as he most certainly has mine.

Downs & Ups

We are in!

Finally, finally, we have moved into the house. Okay, so all we have by way of furniture so far is a new bed (bliss!), a couple of grotty old armchairs that had seen better days even before storage in the barns and the inevitable absorption of the aroma of "eau de goat", and a small patio set to make do for dining. But I don't care. I can even handle the fact that all the parrots are once again caged and objecting loudly about it in the spare room, where a complete lack of soft furnishings allows the din to echo all around the house. As long as that particular measure is a temporary one, that is.

All furniture is on order, and should arrive imminently - although we are never allowed to forget that this is a country that doesn't really have a word for imminently, given that they even use ahora (now) to mean some time in the next fortnight, possibly.

The dogs are settled in their new area, with access to an out-house for shelter from inclement weather and a shady passage behind the house for retreat from fierce sun. I am hoping to get the new parrot flights reconstructed outside very soon. If I can beg, cajole and blackmail John sufficiently, that is.

Reconstructed?

I believe I said in April that we have had no rain this year. I lied.

The non-existent April showers failed to make way for pretty May flowers, and instead we have been treated throughout May and some part of June to tropical rainforest monsoon-style deluges.

The camino, running as it does with a gentle slope downwards from town towards the valley, and then dropping sharply riverward just above our land, has itself become a riverbed, and torrents of water that have collected in the undrained streets of the town have been flowing in great volume and at high speed towards everything we own.

Great swathes of mud move with this water, to be deposited unceremoniously wherever the fancy takes it, usually somewhere where we have just finished clearing a path, or laying out weed barrier, or (in the case of the parrot flights) building the brick roosts at the back of the flights. One fierce and prolonged downpour brought such a wave of water and mud down upon us from the camino that the newly-built roosts were all summarily flattened.

There is nothing worse than having to pick up the shattered pieces of something newly-created and then destroyed, and starting again – and John, who was never enthusiastic about the flights in the first place, has been like a bear with a sore head. So the big clear-up, and the subsequent recommencement from scratch of the work, is being undertaken with heavy hearts and leaden limbs.

It also means that we are going to have to spend more money on some heavy engineering works to divert the watercourse and send it down a safer and less intrusive track.

To top it all, I have just received a letter from the Ayuntamiento (who have been, please note, too busy during the last eight months with fiestas and other such matters of import to send out the formal notification of our sanction for illegal building) saying that they are writing to let me know that they are now very late with said notification and therefore will need to re-initialise the whole procedure.

This does not sound to me to be a move destined to have our interests at heart, so I made haste to the Oficina Técnica to query it.

"It won't change anything," Matías there assures me, "Don't worry!"

I worry. A lot.

"But what if they change their minds after all this time and decide that it can't stand? After all the work we've undertaken to finish it, which we did with the assurance of the Concejal that it is okay to do so?"

Matías again says that nothing will change, but he sees that I remain unconvinced, so he suggests that I write a letter of reply saying that we accept the original decision without the need for reassessment, and that we are ready and willing to pay the fine just as soon as they raise it formally.

I obediently do this – but it is true to say that I now feel that I have the sword of Damocles hanging over my head, given my increasing awareness of the Spanish duplicity, deviousness and general ability to chop and change like the weather – especially the politicians and lawmakers. So I must admit that I would welcome with open arms, as I would never before have thought possible, a written penalty demand for many thousands of euros…

Still.

Glass half full, and all that.

I am determined to remain very positive in the face of the myriad setbacks we seem to encounter as we stumble innocently along our path of discovery in this glorious and strange country.

There is no doubt that we live an immensely interesting (okay, and challenging, too) life here. We are living in the very bosom of nature, surprisingly harsh but astonishingly beautiful, and with the most spectacular backdrop. We are fortunate enough to share this little patch with our motley crew of much-loved animals, and we can afford them plenty of space and freedom to be happy. We also have the honour of a great many amazing wild creatures on our doorstep, including, for instance, a short-toed eagle that clearly has a weather eye on a parrot breakfast, a few dozen firmly entrenched and cheeky little lizards in the outhouses, a couple of hoopoes that spend their entire time telling us to go forth and multiply, a colony of wild black cats that live in small caves in the lower terraces and come up to steal all the cat biscuits left out for Smokie and Ash, to say nothing of all the various sizes and colours of snakes and countless spiders, scorpions (for which I have developed a keen radar), and all the campo creatures that we only ever hear and never see.

We are soon going to make a concerted effort to start on the next construction project, being the hen houses, and to set up the raised beds so that we can plant in earnest the vegetable plots, and in this way increase our level of self-sufficiency another couple of notches.

We will then start stripping out all the old, dead almond trees and ploughing the terraces, in order to bring them back to some semblance of order and to plant young olive trees, to pretend that we are proper farmers who are knowledgeable about and capable of executing such things (although the locals will not be fooled, and will, I am sure, have plenty to say about what we are doing wrong every step of the way!)

Life is suddenly a great deal more luxurious than it has been for well over a year, and on the whole, when I look at it, is for us the pleasurable and fulfilling experience for which, after all, we are each and every one of us constantly striving.

I am blessed.

About Debbie Fletcher

Deborah Fletcher (1958 – still alive and kicking back).

In summary, I suppose I must admit that I am someone who never really had much of a clue about what it is I wanted in life, and so I lurch clumsily through it along a haphazard path in the blind faith that it'll all be fine in the end!

From entering University in 1977 to study pharmacy and then changing my mind and the course of study to biology after a year; from teaching for eight years in FE Colleges and then completely retraining in accountancy and taxation; from running my own accountancy practice for ten years and then selling the whole shooting match to retrain in professional interior design; from living my whole life in England working with papers and rules and then moving to Spain and finding my own brand of anarchy.

All experiences make us what we are. I am clearly a somewhat random cocktail, then!

But I can say truthfully that I have always given everything my best shot, that the milestones in my life are things of which I am proud (my husband, my son, my friends, my assorted ragbag of diverse achievements, my honesty, my creeds), and that I wouldn't, in retrospect, change a damn thing. And at twenty years of age, I'm pretty certain I wouldn't have wanted to grow my own organic produce, keep hens, write a book, make crystal jewellery and run a chaotic menagerie... but here I am after all, as happy as a rotund pink animal in the dubious brown stuff.

I am blessed.

A BRIT'S SCRAPBOOK

GOING NATIVE IN MURCIA

SECOND EDITION

The Essential Guide for Visitors, Expats & Homebuyers

MARCUS JENKINS
DEBBIE JENKINS

FREE FLIGHTS TO BE WON

www.nativespain.com

NativeSpain.com

Spain

2008 *the expat survival guide*

Yolanda Solo

www.nativespain.com

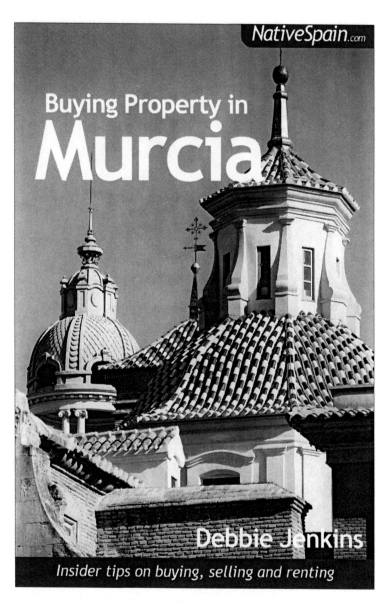

NativeSpain.com

Buying Property in
Murcia

Debbie Jenkins

Insider tips on buying, selling and renting

www.nativespain.com

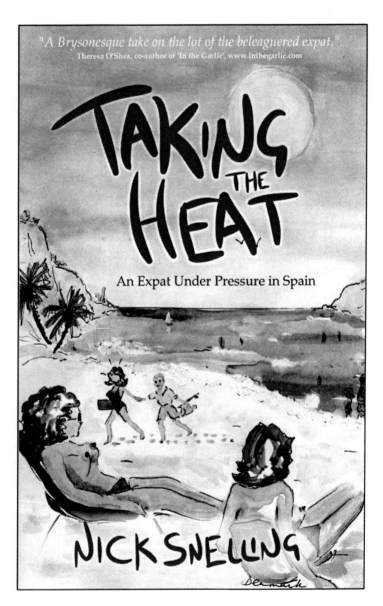

"*A Brysonesque take on the lot of the beleaguered expat.*"
Theresa O'Shea, co-author or 'In the Garlic', www.inthegarlic.com

TAKING THE HEAT

An Expat Under Pressure in Spain

NICK SNELLING

www.nativespain.com

Asociación Protectora de Animales

Dog Rescue and Charity

Caravaca y Cehegín

Our rescue has been in existence since 2003, helping stray and abandoned dogs from Caracava, Cehegín and the surrounding areas. The work was begun by Marisé Checa, a lady from Caravaca, and is now continued by a small, dedicated group of Spanish and British volunteers who give up much of their spare time to the cause.

The Mayor of Cegehín has temporarily given us a small, abandoned house with some land but there is no electricity and all water has to be taken there in bottles. Nevertheless, all of our dogs are well cared for and exercised daily.

Marisé Checa relies totally on voluntary donations and funds are very limited: we have to ensure that we can provide adequate food, shelter and regular vet care, as well as dealing with unforeseen emergency treatment for sick or injured dogs. You can help us financially by making a donation online or sponsoring/virtually adopting a dog.

All of the money goes solely to care for the dogs.

Daily, we help dogs that have been living on the streets, mis-treated or abandoned. Our dogs love being with people and get excited when we go to see them. They really all deserve the chance of a good home, with lots of affection and fun. Please take a moment to look at our web site to see if there is a dog who captures your heart!

www.dogslookingforahome.com

Lightning Source UK Ltd.
Milton Keynes UK
26 January 2010

149123UK00001B/17/P